The New Provençal Cuisine

INNOVATIVE RECIPES FROM THE SOUTH OF FRANCE

by LOUISA JONES

Photography by ALISON HARRIS

Foreword by AUGUSTE AND PIERRE ESCOFFIER

Afterword by FRANÇOIS MILLO
on the Wines of Provence

CHRONICLE BOOKS

SAN FRANCISCO

Library of Congress Cataloging-in-Publication Data available.

Printed in China

Cover and interior design by Palomine.

ISBN 0-8118-0800-9

Distributed in Canada by Raincoast Books
8680 Cambie Street, Vancouver, B.C. V6P 6M9

10 9 8 7 6 5 4 3 2

Chronicle Books
275 Fifth Street
San Francisco, CA 94103

For my ÉMINENCE GRISE

Warm thanks to all the chefs and restaurant owners who so generously received author and photographer, and offered not only their expertise but also their enthusiasm; to my patient husband; to gastronome Christian Millan for his valuable help and advice; to Leslie Stoker for her unfailing support; to Sheila Mooney for being there when I needed her. To the Escoffier family and to François Millo for their generous participation. And to all the team at Chronicle Books, particularly Jacqueline Killeen, who has been much more than a copy editor. For the use of their lovely accessories, the photographer would like to thank Tuile aux Loups, 35 rue Daubenton, 75005 Paris; La Maison Ivre, 38 rue Jacob, 75006 Paris; and Terre de Provence, 26 rue de la Republique; 8400 Avignon as well as to Alice Brinton, Anne Harris, Catherine Healey, and Gloria Spivak.

Contents

Foreword

ESCOFFIER ON THE CULINARY TREASURES OF PROVENCE

"At a time when everything is in constant flux, it would be unreasonable to claim to fix the future of culinary art once and for all . . ." So wrote chef Auguste Escoffier in the preface to his gastronomic guide, which he revised five times between 1903 and 1920, and which has been translated into every current Western language as well as Japanese. Still highly revered by young chefs in Provence, Escoffier was singularly farsighted. In 1909, year of his professional jubilee, he stated: "I often hear it said that chefs' cuisine is declining, whereas in fact it is constantly progressing. If it is true that our stomachs can no longer absorb the meals of earlier generations, it is up to the professionals to adapt to changing customs . . ." In 1934 he added, "The extremely active pace of life today does not allow us to take proper care of our bodies . . . Nature has given us the best of basic ingredients, it is up to the chefs to make best use of their health-giving qualities." It is perhaps this awareness of his public's needs that has made Auguste Escoffier a model for so many young cooks today. And it was above all Escoffier who made the chef de cuisine a serious professional and a public figure, conscious always of the words of the great Parisian chef Antonin Carême (1784–1833): "In cooking there are no principles except that of giving satisfaction."

Escoffier was a Provençal born and bred—the house where he was born in Villeneuve-Loubet has been turned into a charming museum. Although later catering to a cosmopolitan and urban clientele, he never forgot his own

terroir—nor did he look down on its treasures like so many other gastronomes of his time because its cuisine was based on humble olive oil. Late in his life, Escoffier still praised garlic for both flavor and health, judging that even society ladies would appreciate it if there were not a cultural prejudice against it.

The following undated text was discovered as a handwritten fragment among the papers collected by the Fondation Escoffier at Villeneuve-Loubet. It evokes only a few of the region's riches, but with an obvious love of the land and its products.

—Pierre Escoffier, 1993

FROM AVIGNON TO MONTE CARLO

Thanks to its lovely natural settings and its mild climate, Provence has proven a country blessed by the gods.

Its soil supplies gourmands and gourmets with excellent truffles, exquisite wines, savory fruits to be dried or candied. Castellane offers us its prunes, Cavaillon its refreshing melons and delicious white beans, Lauris its asparagus and the rustic olive tree with its silver foliage and its oil, so universally acclaimed; for, without this ingredient, there would be no subtle salad dressings nor smooth mayonnaise.

The dainty and intelligent bee provides her honey, gathered from all the aromatic plants of the countryside. Slopes covered with fragrant herbs as well as salt marshes produce flavorful mutton, whose roasted legs reign in heady majesty at every holiday table, among plates of white beans or the delicate lentil from Saint-Maximin.

And what of the milk-fed lamb, whose plump, pinky-white meat delights all those visitors who come to Provence during its mild and pleasant winters?

When the hunting season comes round, hares, red partridge, woodcocks, thrushes, wild ducks, teal, scoters, ortolans, and quails mingle their rich aromas with the perfumes of the truffle to provide good roasts, *salmis,* and savory stews . . .

A quick look at the blue harvest of the Mediterranean reveals just as many treasures, from the tiny *nonat* or goby which a brilliant and virgin oil transforms into golden sequins; from the delicate sardine from Nice, to the sea bream of the Lerins islands off Cannes. The shiny red rock mullet, after patiently passing through the trials of the barbecue, arrives on the table on a bed of buttered rosemary sprinkled with sea salt and fresh-ground pepper,

fines herbes, and to conclude, a simple chopped shallot and a sprinkling of lemon juice to intensify its flavor.

Or again, those lovely spiny lobsters from Saint-Raphaël which lend themselves so generously to so many culinary preparations. Their flesh is much more delicate than lobster, with a completely different taste . . .

Leaving the sunny shores of the Mediterranean, we can follow the flowery paths that lead to the foothills of the Alps. Here you can fish trout to your heart's content, that pretty creature whose back is covered with tiny pink stars. This is the pearl of our rivers, whose clear waters spring from the flanks of the mountain to fall in silvery cascades on rocky beds. Like the forkbeard (queen of Mediterranean fish) before it appears on the tables of royalty, the trout cries out for limpid and pure olive oil.

And yet, the trout does not disdain to bathe for a few minutes in a court-bouillon of rosé wine, carefully enriched with herbs. And to show itself worthy of princely tastes, it will allow itself to be presented on a bed of parsley, with a crayfish coulis or a mild and foamy sea urchin sauce.

A brief stop in the ancient city of Grasse allows you to inhale the heady essences of roses, jasmine, and violets distilled there for the perfume industry. Do not forget to take away some lovely candied violets and rose petals which are a specialty of the town, and which perfume the breath so delicately.

After this long pilgrimmage in the midst of so many culinary marvels, one arrives at Monte Carlo, the land of golden dreams, where all the treasures of Provence and indeed of the entire world can be found in one place.

—Auguste Escoffier

Hitherto unpublished text by chef Auguste Escoffier. Presented by and made available thanks to the generosity of his grandson, Pierre Escoffier, president of the Fondation Escoffier at Villeneuve-Loubet.

Introduction

The New Provençal Cuisine   IN RECENT YEARS, FRENCH FOOD HAS UNDERGONE A QUIET REVOLUTION. WHILE THE MEDICAL WORLD LAUDS THE VIRTUES OF OLIVE OIL, FISH, FRESH PRODUCE, AND HERBS, FRENCH GASTRONOMY IS ALSO HEADING IN THE SAME DIRECTION, SOUTH TO THE LAND WHERE THIS HEALTHFUL WAY OF EATING ORIGINATES. PROVENÇAL CUISINE TODAY COMBINES THE HERITAGE OF OTHER MEDITERRANEAN COUNTRIES, SUCH AS ITALY, WITH FRENCH ARTISTRY AND *SAVOIR VIVRE*. TODAY'S COOKING IN PROVENCE IS BEING REINVENTED BY AN ENTIRE GENERATION OF YOUNG CHEFS FOR WHOM IT IS FRESH, SEASONAL, QUICKLY PREPARED, FESTIVE, AND CONVIVIAL.   THIS REDISCOVERY OF ANCIENT ROOTS IS NOT MERELY FASHIONABLE AND SUPERFICIAL, AS WAS THE OLD NOUVELLE CUISINE—NOW UNANIMOUSLY CONDEMNED FOR ITS FRIVOLITIES BY THE YOUNG GENERATION. TRADITIONAL SOURCES ARE ENLARGED AND ENRICHED BY COSMOPOLITAN INFLUENCES, FROM NORTH AFRICA OR ASIA AS

WELL AS BY PERSONAL CREATIVITY. ABOVE ALL, THIS STYLE IS ADAPTED TO THE RHYTHMS OF LIFE TODAY. ☀ FOR GENERATIONS, GASTRONOMES DISMISSED PROVENÇAL CUISINE WITH A SHRUG AS INFERIOR BECAUSE OF ITS HUMBLE RESOURCES. "AFTER ALL," RAN THE POPULAR RHETORIC, "PROVENCE IS TOO POOR A COUNTRY TO PRODUCE GOOD FOOD. THERE ARE NO RICH GRASSLANDS FOR CATTLE TO FEED ON, NO BUTTER, AND NO CREAM. ALL THE COOKING IS BASED ON OLIVE OIL, WHICH CAN NEVER HAVE MORE THAN REGIONAL INTEREST. PROVENÇAL CUISINE IS AUSTERE, PEASANT FOOD," THESE CRITICS MAINTAINED. "THE ONLY MEAT IS LAMB, FORCED TO FEED ON POOR SCRUBLAND WHERE ONLY AROMATIC PLANTS LIKE WILD THYME AND ROSEMARY CAN THRIVE. OTHERWISE, PEOPLE SURVIVE ON FISH—FRESH ON THE COAST, DRIED OR SALTED INLAND. AND VEGETABLES, OF COURSE—LOTS OF THOSE, AS ALWAYS IN THE CUISINE OF POOR COUNTRIES. AND FRUIT—WHY, EVEN THE DESSERTS OF CHRISTMAS ARE, FOR THE MOST PART, DRIED RAISINS, ALMONDS, AND APRICOTS! THERE IS VERY LITTLE TRADITIONAL PASTRY IN PROVENCE, AND WHAT THERE IS USES OIL RATHER THAN BUTTER, HONEY RATHER THAN SUGAR, AND ALL THOSE ALMONDS!" ☀ GARLIC, OF COURSE, WAS MUCH SCORNED AS A SOURCE OF PERPETUAL INDIGESTION, IF NOT INDELICATE ODORS. IT WAS JOKINGLY CALLED "THE PROVENÇAL TRUFFLE," AS IF NO OTHER TRUFFLES WORTHY OF THE NAME COULD BE FOUND IN THE REGION! ☀ OCCASIONALLY, HOWEVER, FAMOUS VOICES TOOK UP THE DEFENSE OF POOR PROVENCE. BRITISH NOVELIST FORD MADOX FORD PRAISED ITS FRUGAL FARE AS THE KEY TO LONG LIFE AND WELL-BEING. FRENCH WRITER COLETTE, LIKE FORD, SCORNED THE NORTHERN TOURIST IN SEARCH OF STEAK AND POTATOES, WHOSE DOCTOR (IN THOSE DAYS) FORBAD GARLIC AND OIL-BASED CUISINE AS INJURIOUS TO THE HEALTH, ADDING: "I WILL FOREVER PRAISE THE EXCELLENCE OF ANY OLD PROVENÇAL DISH, THE VIRTUES OF GARLIC, THE TRANSCENDENCE OF OLIVE OIL." SHE INSISTED ON HER LOYALTY TO THOSE THREE, BRIGHTLY COLORED VEGETABLES: EGGPLANTS, TOMATOES, AND

SWEET PEPPERS. ☀ BOTH THESE CHALLENGES TO PREVAILING OPINION WERE WRITTEN AROUND 1930. BOTH WRITERS SPENT A LOT OF TIME ON THE FRENCH RIVIERA, AND BOTH TURNED UP THEIR NOSES AT THE COSMOPOLITAN SETTLERS, PRETENTIOUS AND NOUVEAU RICHE, WHO SPENT WADS OF MONEY ON FANCY FOOD IN OPULENT RESTAURANTS WHILE SCORNING SIMPLE COUNTRY FARE. ☀ SO IT IS THAT, FOR GENERATIONS, PROVENÇAL RESTAURANT COOKING WAS CAUGHT BETWEEN TWO CURRENTS OF OPINION: DISMISSED BY THE FRENCH GASTRONOMIC ESTABLISHMENT ON THE ONE HAND AS TOO PEASANTLIKE, AND BY LOVERS OF AUTHENTIC COUNTRY FARE AS TOO PRETENTIOUS. ELIZABETH DAVID, WRITING SOME THIRTY YEARS LATER, DESCRIBES WITH REGRETFUL COMPASSION THE COMPROMISES FORCED ON ANY PEASANT'S SON WHO TURNS INTO A FAMOUS CHEF (A PORTRAIT MODELED ON ESCOFFIER). COMES THE DAY WHEN HE WISHES TO REPRODUCE A RUSTIC DISH OF HIS CHILDHOOD: SLICED POTATOES AND ARTICHOKE HEARTS BAKED WITH OLIVE OIL AND GARLIC AND SCENTED WITH WILD THYME. HE CANNOT, HE FEELS, OFFER SUCH SIMPLE FARE TO HIS ELEGANT PUBLIC; HE MUST REPLACE THE GARLIC WITH TRUFFLES—ALSO A COUNTRY INGREDIENT, BUT HIS PATRONS WILL NOT KNOW THAT. OLIVE OIL WILL NOT BE ACCEPTABLE TO PARISIANS OR LONDONERS, SO BUTTER IS SUBSTITUTED. MEAT JUICE ENRICHES THE SAUCE—FOR IN THOSE DAYS, EVERY SERIOUS KITCHEN KEPT ITS SUPPLY OF MEAT ESSENCES AND STOCKS AT THE READY TO ADD TO EVERYTHING. AND WHILE THE CHEF'S POOR PROVENÇAL FAMILY MIGHT ORIGINALLY HAVE MADE A WHOLE MEAL OF THIS DISH, WITH THE ADDITION OF A SAUCERFUL OF OLIVES AND SOME FIGS FOR DESSERT, THE GREAT RESTAURANT CHEF IS OBLIGED TO ADD WITH A JOINT OF MEAT. AND HE NAMES THE DISH *CARRÉ D'AGNEAU MISTRAL*, AND PRINTS THE RECIPE IN HIS COOKBOOK. AFTER THIS THE GASTRONOMIC ESTABLISHMENT TAKES IT SERIOUSLY ENOUGH TO DEBATE WHICH BORDEAUX VINTAGE MIGHT BEST ACCOMPANY THE LAMB, THE POTATOES, AND THE ARTICHOKES. ☀ PRAISE BE, THOSE DAYS ARE GONE. TODAY, ALL SERIOUS CHEFS

CONCUR THAT PROVENCE PROVIDES A PARTICULARLY RICH RANGE OF RAW MATERIALS FOR SERIOUS CUISINE—SOME HAVE BEEN KNOWN TO MOVE SOUTH PRIMARILY FOR THIS REASON. IN FRANCE, THE RIVIERA IS NOW SECOND ONLY TO THE PARISIAN REGION FOR ITS HOST OF GOOD RESTAURANTS. PATRONS TODAY ARE OF COURSE ONLY TOO HAPPY TO EAT OIL-BASED CUISINE. WHAT WAS ONCE DISMISSED AS "FRUGAL" OR "AUSTERE" IS NOW PRAISED AS "LIGHT"—INFINITELY BETTER FOR THE HEALTH. INSTEAD OF ENRICHING PEASANT DISHES WITH BUTTER AND MEAT JUICE, TODAY'S CHEFS ADD A FAR MORE PRECIOUS INGREDIENT— IMAGINATION. PEASANT FOOD, OR GRANDMOTHER'S FARE, OR JUST HOME COOKING PROVIDES THE VERY BASIS OF THE NEW PROVENÇAL CUISINE, WHICH HAS AN EDGE ON OTHER REGIONAL CUISINES PRECISELY BECAUSE IT IS BASED NOT ON BUTTER, BUT ON THAT FRAGRANT AND LIFE-GIVING NECTAR, OLIVE OIL. IN THE SOUTH, AS IN PARIS, MANY FINE CHEFS SALUTE THE TRADITIONAL, GRASSROOTS COOKING BY PROVIDING IT EITHER IN A SEPARATE ESTABLISHMENT (A BISTRO), OR FOR SPECIAL MENUS, OR ON ONE NIGHT A WEEK, OR WHATEVER. BUT IT IS STILL TRUE TODAY THAT CHEFS ARE ARTISTS, AND THEIR PATRONS WANT FROM THEM SOMETHING MORE PERSONAL, MORE INIMITABLE THAN THE FAMILIAR, OLD-FASHIONED DISHES. TODAY'S YOUNG CHEFS EXCEL IN TWO RESPECTS: THEIR ABILITY TO SEEK OUT THE VERY FINEST INGREDIENTS OF THE LOCAL *TERROIR* AND THEIR CAPACITY FOR INVENTING ORIGINAL WAYS OF ENHANCING COUNTRY SAVORS—NOT BY THE ADDITION OF LUXURY INGREDIENTS THAT MASK AND WEIGH DOWN THE DISH, BUT BY NEW TASTE COMBINATIONS. IN OTHER WORDS, BY PERSONAL CREATIVITY WITH THE RAW MATERIALS THEMSELVES AND WITH THE COUNTRY TRADITIONS THEY HAVE ALREADY INSPIRED. AT THE SAME TIME, THEIR LINK WITH THE *TERROIR*, THE PRODUCE OF THE LAND, IS STRONGER THAN EVER. THE WINES THAT SUIT THESE CREATIONS ARE NOT BORDEAUX OR BURGUNDIES, BUT THOSE THAT SPRING FROM THE SAME SOIL AS THE FOOD ITSELF, THE WINES OF PROVENCE, AND PARTICULARLY THE

FAST-DEVELOPING APPELLATIONS GROUPED UNDER THE TITLE OF CÔTES DE PROVENCE. WHAT, THEN, ARE THE MAIN CHARACTERISTICS OF PROVENÇAL COOKING TODAY, BESIDES ITS EMPHASIS ON OLIVE OIL, FISH, FRESH FRUIT, AND VEGETABLES? EACH DISH CONTAINS A SKILLFUL BALANCE OF TEXTURES AS WELL AS FLAVORS, AND IT IS THE ORIGINAL COMBINING OF SIMPLE INGREDIENTS THAT CREATES APPEAL. THERE NO LONGER ARE COMPLICATED SAUCES— LONG-SIMMERED AFFAIRS WITH MEAT GLAZES—BUT VERY SIMPLE, FAST REDUCTIONS OF THE COOKING JUICES USED IN THE DISH ITSELF. STOCKS AND BROTHS ARE MADE WITH THE BONES OF THE FISH OR MEAT TO BE SERVED OR WITH THE VEGETABLE COOKING WATER. IN SOME CASES, THE VERY VEGETABLE PARINGS ARE SIMMERED TO PROVIDE A SAUCE BASE—AN ECONOMY THE CONTEMPORARY HOME COOK WILL CERTAINLY APPRECIATE! THIS IS NOT, HOWEVER, FAT-FREE FOOD, ALTHOUGH IT IS GENERALLY MUCH LIGHTER THAN OLD-STYLE FRENCH CUISINE. FAT, AFTER ALL, ADDS PRECIOUS FLAVOR AND TEXTURE. ACTUAL COOKING METHODS USE MOSTLY OIL, AND KEEP IT TO A MINIMUM, BUT BUTTER AND CREAM MAY STILL BE ADDED AS A FINAL ENRICHMENT. VEGETABLES TODAY ARE INVARIABLY COOKED FOR A VERY SHORT TIME IN LARGE POTS OF BOILING, SALTED WATER, THEN DIPPED INTO ICE WATER TO STOP FURTHER COOKING. THUS FLAVOR, COLOR, AND TEXTURE ARE BEST PRESERVED. MEAT AND FISH ROASTS ARE USUALLY BROWNED FIRST, THEN FINISHED QUICKLY IN A HOT OVEN. NONE OF THESE RECIPES INVOLVES LONG BAKING, ROASTING, OR SIMMERING. MOST INVOLVE VERY SIMPLE, LAST-MINUTE COOKING. THE MOST COMPLICATED AMONG THEM MAY REQUIRE SEVERAL SUCH SIMPLE PREPARATIONS, AND THE ONLY DIFFICULTY ENCOUNTERED BY THE HOME COOK MAY BE LAST-MINUTE TIMING AND ASSEMBLY. AS FOR THE DESSERTS, THEY ARE FRUIT BASED, UNLESS VEGETABLES OR AROMATIC HERBS REPLACE THE FRUIT. ICE CREAMS AND SORBETS ARE CHERISHED. PASTRY IS RARELY MORE THAN A GARNISH. INDEED, FLOUR IS A RARE INGREDIENT ANYWHERE IN THIS CUISINE, AND SUGAR IS KEPT TO A MINIMUM.

This is family-style cooking. Even male chefs often acknowledge a debt to mothers and home cooks generally in their inspiration. Produce is purchased and food is prepared in small batches even in restaurants, and imagination is stimulated by what each day's market has to offer. Most chefs aspire also to the best kind of family atmosphere, a convivial dialogue with customers, the pleasure of giving pleasure. Even some of the most famous dream of a small country restaurant seating only forty to eighty diners. Unfortunately, times are hard and very competitive even in the golden land of Provence. This world is highly mobile. This book is intended to capture a particular moment, but if individuals change places as their careers progress, the general trend only grows in strength. For all of these chefs are artists, taking great pride in their profession. Some are already stars in French gastronomy, like Jean-André Charial of the Oustau de Baumnière and Jacques Chibois, just opening his own country inn at Grasse. Some shun the limelight, preferring the security of a hotel setting. Of course, the fifteen selected here are not the only talented chefs of the region. Many others could easily have been cited. All share a deep seriousness about their art, a great respect for fresh, seasonal raw materials, a high regard for country traditions as well as for international exchange, and a desire to break out of the pretentious trappings of old-fashioned French gastronomy to achieve a new simplicity. In this, they have wonderfully succeeded. The following chapters have been organized to allow easy traveling down the Rhône valley to Avignon, with visits in all directions from this hub city; then eastward to Aix and Marseille, up the coast beyond Nice, and finally inland toward the Riviera backcountry at Grasse. Much as in Auguste Escoffier's vision of the Provençal *terroir* unfolding its riches.

17

Taste Tests in Avignon

MENU

BELGIAN ENDIVE AND ANCHOVY SALAD
Saladette d'endives aux anchois

FRESH COD VINAIGRETTE WITH SEA SALT
Morue vinaigrette à la fleur de sel

SADDLE OF RABBIT WITH HONEY AND LEMON
Rable de lapin au miel et au citron

CHOCOLATE DELIGHT PLATE
Assiette tout chocolat

CHRISTIAN ETIENNE   *Restaurant Christian Etienne*   AVIGNON

Avignon has been a great crossroads since prehistoric times. It is strategically located at the junction of two great rivers (the Rhône and the Durance) and not far from the Mediterranean. For many centuries, the silhouette of its medieval towers and belfries etched against the blue Provençal sky has beckoned to visitors and pilgrims from afar, "like a galleon in full sail," writes Lawrence Durrell, "across the mistral-scourged plain." The contemporary city has kept its long, crenellated ramparts encircling the old part of town. The Palace of the Popes dominates this skyline, built in just twenty years for the series of popes who resided here throughout the fourteenth century. Today it still stands, an imposing mass of luminous limestone (flecked with ancient seashells), in the heart of the medieval city. The palace is said to be the second most visited monument in provincial France.

The magnificent gothic chapel of Pope Clement VI at its south end was such an ambitious project that its architects were obliged to construct an enormous, thick, stone buttress over the winding, picturesque street below (the Rue Peyrollerie). This support still stands solidly on the hard, bare rock that underlies all this sec-

tion of the city. And right next to the buttress, as practically an extension of the papal palace, is an elegant, fourteenth-century building, restored and converted in 1990 into Avignon's best restaurant. This is the home of Christian Etienne.

Christian Etienne's setting is worthy of its illustrious neighbor. He, too, has fourteenth-century frescoes depicting coats of arms all along one wall of the dining room. And in his way, he continues the artistic tradition of Simone Martini and the other Siennese painters commissioned by the popes. Etienne is the very model of the professional chef as artist: conscientious but gregarious, ambitious but also a bit of a dreamer, well organized but adaptable, very serious about his work but loving a good joke. Today, of course, Etienne's patrons are not popes but the establishment of Avignon (a city that regards him with great pride), the directors and stars of the summer theater festival, local associations or families celebrating special events, and—the chef is wont to say with a rueful smile—his banker. About 80 percent of his customers are local, in spite of tough competition from the classic and infallible Hiély-Lucullus just down the street, or other talented young chefs like Robert Brunel. More and more, however, travelers from all over the world are drawn by Etienne's fast-growing reputation.

Steps lead up to the restaurant's broad, outdoor terrace, from which one can watch the whole spectacle of the square of the Place du Palais (lit up and lively in the evenings) or admire the recent portraits of theater personalities painted on the walls of buildings across the street. Or simply concentrate on the food, which deserves in itself complete attention.

Christian Etienne was born in Avignon and went off on the usual tour of apprenticeship, spending time at the Ritz in Paris, where he mastered a number of Escoffier's recipes. The young chef has learned his classics and watched the demise of nouvelle cuisine with some relief. Etienne returned to Avignon and set up a small

restaurant in the old town. The team he still works with today was also with him there, a solid and loyal group to which he attributes much of his success. ("We often don't need to speak, a look is enough.") When the ruined building the restaurant now inhabits came up for sale, Etienne moved heaven and earth (with the blessing of papal ghosts?) to get it. His mother claims that once, when she took him walking as a child in the gardens of the Palace of the Popes, he pointed out this building to her and said he would live there one day. However that may be, the site, as renovated, suits him admirably, a blend of tradition and modernity similar to his cuisine.

Part of the appeal at Christian Etienne's is the atmosphere of festive conviviality, of youthful enthusiasm. He himself has an expansive, easy gaiety in spite of working under intense pressure. He possesses that quality that novelist Alphonse Daudet described as "the

tremendous prodigality with which the southerner expends his whole being."

Etienne's customers trust him and think of him as a genial host. They know he works from a solid base ("Cooking is like music; you have to know your scales, but after that you depend a lot on feeling.") He encourages his team to read old cookbooks. At the same time, he guides them with a strong sense of professional ethics, respect for the customer, respect for the product.

The inventive part comes after a trip to Avignon's market, when Christian Etienne brings home the day's finds. He experiments constantly, and his menus reflect his originality. He goes through phases, he feels, and at the moment is trying out different bouillons. The results may be a dish of scallops *en nage de truffes* with carrots and wood mushrooms, and fried parsley for a texture contrast; or a pigeon pot-au-feu flavored with lovage. He worked with steam for a while but now uses it less and less. He prefers his fish roasted, as do many of his contemporaries. Not everything works out, however; Etienne spent a lot to time working with persimmons, but did not find a way of cooking them without increasing their astringency. He had better results in trials with wild blackberries.

Vegetables figure largely on Etienne's menus; indeed there is a special *menu des légumes* with a vegetable pot-au-feu, a chard gratin, a potato and olive cake, and a fennel sherbet with saffron sauce. Unusual herbs put in an appearance here as well as in the creamed oysters and lobster with lemon balm or in the pigeon with lovage. His techniques of cooking allow for long, slow preparations (stews and gratins), which most of his colleagues forego for faster methods. But his sauces remain light, usually a blend of natural juices.

An important part of the life of any professional chef is his participation in the many events, competitions, and demonstrations that quickly fill up the calendar of the gastronomic year. The menu given here is a good example of midwinter Provençal cuisine, but it is also the menu that Christian Etienne contributed to a nationwide Week of Savors organized by food critic Christian Millau to promote gastronomic instruction to school children all over the country.

A survey had shocked the French public: Only 12 percent of children interrogated could name the four main taste groups (salt, acid, bitter, and sweet); only 42 percent could name more than three varieties of potatoes; 65 percent did not know the exact composition of a mayonnaise; 77 percent could not identify the smell of fresh vanilla! As a result, *Gault-Millau Magazine* organized a taste week in October, 1992, during which France's most prestigious chefs brought their favorite products to schools.

A Breton chef brought fresh butter, "the real kind, that smells of the cow and gives off drops of water when

you cut it." Christian Etienne brought rare fruits of the Midi: jujubes and persimmons. In each case, the aim was to make children aware of their own *terroir*, their local heritage. In one class, each child got a rare and wonderful gift: a perfectly ripe pear. A Parisian chef brought a jar of caviar and asked how many in the class had already tasted it. One boy said he had it all the time, but it turned out he was thinking of lentils.

Each chef's menu contained the four major taste groups. In Christian Etienne's (following), the chocolate and the endives are bitter, the anchovies and cod are salted, the honey and part of the dessert plate are sweet, and the lemon and vinegar of the two vinaigrettes are acid. It is a good teaching menu. It is also delicious, simple to prepare, and perfectly adapted to family cooking.

BELGIAN ENDIVE
AND ANCHOVY SALAD
Saladette d'endives aux anchois

This recipe is inspired by the old Provençal *anchoïade* sauce served always with raw vegetables. Etienne has imagined a particularly pretty version.

SERVES 4

4 endives (about $1/2$ pound total), trimmed
1 teaspoon butter
2 anchovy fillets in oil, drained
1 clove garlic, crushed into a paste
1 tablespoon sherry vinegar
6 tablespoons olive oil
Salt and freshly ground black pepper, to taste
1 tablespoon chopped fresh chervil

Cut the tips off the endives about 2 inches from the top; mince finely and reserve. Remove the bitter hearts from the stem ends and discard; reserve leaves.

In a small saucepan, melt the butter and add the anchovy fillets. Cook, stirring, for 1 to 2 minutes, over low heat. Add the crushed garlic and vinegar, and stir to make a homogeneous paste. Remove from heat and beat in 3 tablespoons olive oil, salt, and pepper.

Mix 2 tablespoons of the anchovy mixture with the reserved minced endive tips and make a mound in the center of each of 4 plates. Make a pretty pattern with the remaining olive oil around each mound, and lay out the endive leaves in a petal design. Dribble the rest of the anchovy sauce around the outside. Sprinkle with the chopped chervil and serve.

FRESH COD VINAIGRETTE
WITH SEA SALT
Morue vinaigrette à la fleur de sel

Inspired by the many salt cod dishes traditional in Provençal cooking, this one uses fresh fish, cooked with its skin on in the current fashion. The special sea salt of Brittany, *sel de Guérande*, is not simply a preserving agent here but a condiment, adding its own unique flavor.

SERVES 4

4 cod fillets (about $1/4$ pound each), skin intact
Salt and freshly ground black pepper, to taste
$1 1/2$ cups olive oil plus 1 tablespoon for baking dish
2 tablespoons fresh lemon juice
Small bunch chives, finely chopped
5 sprigs fresh parsley, finely chopped
5 fresh tarragon leaves, finely chopped
5 fresh chervil leaves, finely chopped
6 tablespoons sea salt
2 medium-sized tomatoes, peeled, seeded, and diced

Preheat the oven to 400°F. Sprinkle the cod fillets with fine salt and pepper and place them in an oiled gratin dish just large enough to hold them. Bake until the fish just barely flakes when tested with a fork, 10 to 15 minutes. Set aside.

In a small bowl, mix together the lemon juice, salt, and pepper, then slowly beat in $1 1/2$ cups olive oil to make a vinaigrette.

Remove the skin from the cod; it should pull away easily. Transfer the cod to a serving platter, spoon over the vinaigrette, and sprinkle with chopped herbs and sea salt. Arrange the tomato dice on the side as a garnish. This dish can be served hot or lukewarm.

SADDLE OF RABBIT WITH HONEY AND LEMON
Rable de lapin au miel et au citron

Chef Etienne uses saddle of rabbit here, but the recipe lends itself equally well to chicken breasts. Most butchers will not sell rabbit parts, so it might be necessary to buy whole rabbits and have the butcher bone out and debone the saddles (the most desirable part of the animal). The other parts could then be saved for another dish. Alternatively, whole rabbits could be used, adding more lemon juice, honey, and broth for the sauce, to serve a larger group of people. Either chicken broth or homemade rabbit broth is suitable, the latter prepared from the saddle bones. Once the choice of meat has been made, this dish is very simple, quick to prepare, and uses two Mediterranean country ingredients, lemon and honey, to enhance the meat's own flavor.

SERVES 4

1 lemon
Saddles of 2 rabbits, deboned (about 4 ounces
  each after deboning)
1 tablespoon peanut oil or safflower oil
1 teaspoon honey
3/4 cup rich chicken broth or stock (store-bought
  or page 155)
1/2 stick (4 tablespoons) butter, diced
Salt and freshly ground black pepper, to taste

Preheat the oven to 400°F. Bring a small saucepan of water to a boil. Remove the zest from the lemon in julienne strips, and dip it for 10 seconds into the boiling water. Drain through a sieve and reserve zest.

Cut each rabbit saddle in half lengthwise. Roll up each of the 4 pieces and tie with string. Rub with oil and place them in a roasting pan just large enough to hold them. Bake until golden in color and cooked through so that juices run clear when pricked with a fork, 10 to 15 minutes. Remove the meat from the pan and keep warm, reserving the juices in the pan.

Over low heat, add the honey and the juice of the lemon to the roasting pan and stir, scraping up the brown bits. Pour in the broth and stir again. Add the blanched lemon zest, bring to a low boil, and simmer to reduce the sauce by about half. Beat in the diced butter to thicken. Adjust the seasoning with salt and pepper.

Slice the meat and arrange it in a fan shape on each of 4 warmed serving plates. Spoon over the sauce and serve immediately.

•

CHOCOLATE DELIGHT PLATE
Assiette tout chocolat

This dessert is a delicious medley of classic French elements. The bitter flavor of the chocolate complements the three previous courses, bringing this tasty menu to its logical conclusion.

SERVES 4

CHOCOLATE COULIS
1/4 cup sugar
2 tablespoons water
2 tablespoons heavy cream
2 tablespoons best quality cocoa powder

CHOCOLATE SHERBET TARTS
2 cups water
3/4 cup sugar
6 ounces bittersweet chocolate, broken into bits
1 cup best quality cocoa powder
4 baked tart shells of sweet pastry (store-bought
  or page 154)

CHOCOLATE MOUSSE
4 ounces extra-bitter chocolate, broken into bits
3 eggs, separated
1/3 cup sugar

To Prepare the Chocolate Coulis

Mix together all the ingredients in a small saucepan and heat gently over low heat, stirring constantly. Bring just to the boil, then remove from the heat and leave to cool.

To Prepare the Chocolate Sherbet

Put the water and sugar in a small saucepan. Place over low heat, stirring constantly until the sugar dissolves. Bring to a boil, but do not stir once the boiling point is reached. Simmer gently 5 minutes and remove from the heat. Dissolve the chocolate bits in the hot syrup, stirring to melt.

In a small bowl, make a paste with the cocoa and a few tablespoons of the chocolate sugar syrup. When well blended, gradually beat in the rest of the syrup and mix well. Let cool and freeze in a sherbet maker according to the manufacturer's directions. Just before serving, spoon the sherbet into the baked tart shells.

To Prepare the Chocolate Mousse

Melt the chocolate in the top of a double boiler over simmering water. In a medium-sized bowl, beat together the egg yolks and the sugar with a fork or whisk. Gradually pour the melted chocolate into the yolk mixture, stirring constantly. In a separate bowl, beat the egg whites until stiff peaks form. Fold the whites gently into the yolk and chocolate mixture until homogeneous. Cover and chill.

To Assemble the Dessert

On each of 4 chilled plates, dribble I teaspoon of coulis in a pretty pattern. Arrange on each plate a sherbet tart and a scoop of mousse. Spoon over the remaining coulis before serving.

Spring Bounties

MENU

Spring Vegetable Medley
with Shrimp and Green Pea Cream
Meli-Mélo de légumes printiniers,
langoustines et crème de pois frais

Herbed Salmon Pastries
with Fresh Asparagus
Fines galettes de saumon, asperges vertes,
caviar et herbes fraîches

Roast Chicken with Parsley Butter
Volaille de Bresse simplement rôtie
au beurre de persil

Strawberry Crisps
with White Chocolate Mousse
Croustillant aux fraises et mousse
au chocolat blanc

SERGE CHENET   *Le Prieuré*   VILLENEUVE-LEZ-AVIGNON

Villeneuve-lez-Avignon is the very image of Provençal *douceur de vivre*, "art of living," as it is termed today. This charming community of some ten thousand inhabitants lies just across the Rhône river from the great, humming city of Avignon, but it has a character all its own, much appreciated by both locals and travelers. Old Villeneuve offers all the picturesque appeal of a country village, with winding, cobbled streets decked with trellises and window boxes; and, at the same time, it possesses the elegance and cultural importance of an urban center. The town maintains close ties with Avignon, where many residents of Villeneuve carry on their public and professional lives.

The two communities have faced each other across the broad back of the Rhône for centuries—Villeneuve always observing Avignon's ambitious bustle from its own quiet vantage point. Indeed, thanks to the hills rising steeply on the river's west bank, all parts of the smaller town enjoy stunning views of Avignon's dramatic, medieval skyline.

The heart of old Villeneuve consists of one main street, a market square, and a fourteenth-century church whose belltower marks the hours of quiet days. Right

behind the church is its priory, known as Le Prieuré, now one of France's most beautiful and secluded hotels. It is here that chef Serge Chenet works his magic.

Le Prieuré shares with the rest of Villeneuve an air of old nobility, the result of its distinguished history. Everything began for this community in the eighth century when a holy hermit, Sainte Césarie, lived and died on a high hill nearby. First a shrine, then a monastery grew up on the spot, later named the Abbaye de Saint-André. Today its massive, crenellated fortifications dominate the surrounding houses. The abbey can be visited and its ramparts now shelter a large, steeply terraced Provençal garden, so beautiful that many local couples come here to have their wedding pictures taken. Henry James admired this citadel more than a century ago, lying on his back under an olive tree on a spring afternoon "of a yellow brightness." He wrote that: "It was very soft, very still and pleasant . . . an old city wall for a background, a canopy of olives, and for a couch the soil of Provence."

Until the thirteenth century, the community remained perched on its hilltop. Only then did the "new" town of Villeneuve grow up below. In those days, the town was ruled by the king of France, while the other side of the river still belonged to the counts of Provence. When the popes settled in Avignon as of 1307, and all the cardinals competed in building fine palaces, many chose to settle in the quieter regions across the river. So it is that Villeneuve-lez-Avignon, already in the fourteenth century, became an elegant and urbane bedroom community for the city of Avignon.

The buildings of Le Prieuré and the adjoining church were built for Cardinal Arnaud de Via as of 1333. In 1943, the convent buildings were restored and transformed into a comfortable pension by the Mille family. Although now an elegant and luxurious hotel, it is still managed by the same family.

The Prieuré's gracious gardens provide the ideal

place to celebrate spring in Provence—fruit trees flowering in succession, long-awaited vegetables suddenly available on the markets. Chef Serge Chenet has become an expert in their orchestration. Born in Brittany (another region famous for early spring vegetables), he first came to Le Prieuré in 1975, working here in the summers in a supporting role over a period of years, while spending winter seasons as top chef at a luxury ski resort hotel in Courchevel. He also worked on the Riviera, at the elegant Belles Rives in Juan-les-Pins—seeking always the south and the sun.

Chenet's style perfectly fits the discrete charm of the establishment. Too modest to become a media star himself, he nonetheless strives constantly to learn and evolve, going almost yearly to workshops directed by the great names of the profession: the Troisgros brothers, Georges Blanc, Gaston Lenôtre, Alain Ducasse, Joël Robuchon, or Marc Meneau. His benevolent presence is felt in the affable, efficient organization of his kitchen, which must (as in all hotels) ensure equal quality for breakfast trays and teas, poolside meals and formal dinners. Above all, he has developed his own style of cuisine, guaranteed to delight without fatiguing, to surprise without shocking. This is one of those rare hostelries where one can eat long, sleep well, and be hungry the next day.

Chenet loves to experiment with ingredients such as foie gras served with *épeautre* (winter wheat) and beet cream, with techniques (spiced pigeon cooked in a vacuum pack), with colors (grilled veal with two sauces, one based on tapenade, the other enriched with goat cheese, arranged on a plate for a marbled effect). But always flavor counts most, directly linked to the quality of the ingredients. He gets many of his raw materials at the Avignon market, but carefully seeks out the best suppliers for each kind of fish, each kind of cheese. The hotel's set menu changes daily, the à la carte listing with the seasons. Provençal sunshine and garden produce light up every line, as in the dish of spring vegetables with truffle juice, or fish with fennel coulis, or lamb with eggplant petals, or prawn-stuffed crêpes with basil *pommade*.

Chenet particularly excels at sensing his public's wishes, whether it be Japanese guests who want a number of small dishes and no cheese, Americans who long for mixed salads, or ambitious gastronomes in search of adventure. In the old Prieuré tradition, he is first attentive to his public, then inventive about meeting its desires and needs. The following menu is a perfect example; it lives and breathes spring in Provence, but its recipes, while delighting the eye and the palate, remain simple to prepare, designed with the home cook in mind.

SPRING VEGETABLE MEDLEY
WITH SHRIMP AND
GREEN PEA CREAM
Meli-Mélo de légumes printiniers, langoustines et crème de pois frais

This dish can be composed of any number of tender young vegetables according to market choice and personal preference.

SERVES 4

2 quarts water
Salt and freshly ground black pepper, to taste
Juice of 1/2 lemon
5 or 6 selections from the following vegetables:
    4 artichoke hearts or whole baby artichokes
    4 new carrots with their leaves
    4 small zucchini with blossoms if possible
    4 pearl onions
    1/4 pound thin green beans
    1 stalk celery, cut into 4 or 5 pieces
    1/2 fennel, tough outer leaves removed and
       bulb cut into 4 pieces
    4 small, young turnips with their leaves
    4 young leaves of green cabbage
    4 fresh mushrooms caps
    4 cauliflower florets, trimmed
6 tablespoons butter
White part of 1 leek, minced
1/2 pound fresh snow peas, trimmed
2 cups chicken broth or stock (store-bought or page 155)
2/3 cup crème fraîche or heavy cream
8 jumbo shrimp, peeled and deveined
1 tablespoon olive oil

In a large saucepan, bring the water to a boil with 1 1/2 teaspoons salt and the lemon juice. Cook each of the selected vegetables separately in the boiling water until just tender. Remove the vegetables with a slotted spoon and transfer to a bowl of ice water. Drain and set aside. Keep the pan of hot water simmering.

Melt the butter in a heavy-bottomed, medium-sized saucepan and cook the leek over low heat for 2 minutes. Add the snow peas and chicken broth and season with salt and pepper. Bring to a boil, reduce heat, and simmer until tender, about 10 minutes.

Transfer the snow pea mixture to a blender or food processor and purée until thickened. Strain through a fine sieve into a bowl, return the mixture to the saucepan, and stir in the crème fraîche. Adjust the seasoning. Keep warm over low heat. If necessary, bring to a boil and simmer to reduce slightly, but the mixture should remain fairly liquid.

Sprinkle the shrimp with salt and pepper. Heat the olive oil in a small skillet over medium-high heat, and sauté the shrimp quickly until barely golden and cooked through, about 2 minutes.

Reheat the cooked vegetables by combining them in a sieve or salad basket and dipping them quickly again in the boiling water. Drain the vegetables well and transfer them to a bowl. Toss very carefully with the butter, salt, and pepper.

In the center of each of 4 plates, spread a circle of fresh pea cream. Arrange the vegetables decoratively with 2 shrimp in the center of each circle. Serve immediately.

•

HERBED SALMON PASTRIES
WITH FRESH ASPARAGUS
Fines galettes de saumon, asperges vertes, caviar et herbes fraîches

The town of Lauris in the Luberon is especially famous for its asparagus. In the 1930s, chef Auguste Escoffier encouraged its producers to concentrate on green asparagus, which his customers at the Savoy in

London particularly appreciated. Today both the violet-white and the green varieties are commonly available in the local markets of Provence. Salmon, of course, is not local, but usually imported from Scotland by Provençal restaurants. It does provide a good complement for the asparagus, while the *galette* adds a wonderful crispy texture.

SERVES 4

12 ounces puff pastry (store-bought or page 153)
Butter, at room temperature, for greasing foil
1-pound salmon fillet, cut into 4 round pieces about
  4 inches in diameter
1 tablespoon olive oil, plus more for cookie sheet
Salt and freshly ground black pepper, to taste
16 green asparagus tips
2/3 cup whipping cream
2 tablespoons fresh lemon juice
1 teaspoon strong prepared mustard
4 tablespoons chopped fresh chives
1 tablespoon chopped fresh chervil
1 tablespoon chopped fresh dill
4 teaspoons caviar (optional)

Preheat the oven to 400°F. On a floured surface, roll out the pastry to a 6x3-inch rectangle. From the short side, roll the pastry tightly to make a long roll. Cut the roll into 4 equal pieces. With a rolling pin, flatten each of the pieces into a thin circle 4 inches in diameter. Lay them between 2 sheets of buttered aluminum foil on a cookie sheet, and put another cookie sheet on top. Chill for 20 minutes.

Rub the salmon fillets with olive oil, salt, and pepper. Place them on an oiled cookie sheet.

Peel the asparagus and cut the tip ends into 3-inch lengths. Bring a large pan of heavily salted water to a boil and add the asparagus. Cook until just barely tender, about 10 minutes. Gently remove the asparagus and dip into a bowl filled with ice water. Drain and reserve. Keep the water simmering.

Whip the cream in a large, chilled bowl until soft peaks form. Add the lemon juice, mustard, 2 tablespoons of the chives, salt, and pepper. Cover the bowl with plastic wrap and refrigerate.

Remove the pastry rounds from the regrigerator and remove the top cookie sheet and top sheet of foil. Bake them in the oven until golden brown, 8 to 10 minutes. Add the salmon rounds to the oven for the last 3 minutes. Take care not to overcook the fish.

In a small bowl, mix together 2 tablespoons chives with the chervil and dill. Dip the asparagus quickly in the boiling water to reheat.

Place a pastry round on each of 4 plates. Using a large spatula, carefully place a salmon fillet on each pastry round. Surround each with 4 asparagus tips. Using 2 large tablespoons dipped in boiling water, form 4 evenly shaped oval mounds with the herbed cream and arrange them on the plates. Sprinkle the salmon with the mixed chopped herbs. If you like, on the tip of each cream mound, place a small spoonful of caviar. Serve immediately, for the cream should melt as the dish is eaten.

•

ROAST CHICKEN WITH PARSLEY BUTTER
Volaille de Bresse simplement rôtie au beurre de persil

Although simple in its conception and absolutely delicious, this dish is very rich because of the butter sauce. It requires absolutely first quality ingredients, both for the bird and the butter. Bresse chickens come from the region just north of Provence and are corn fed. If possible, use a corn-fed bird, but at least buy a free-range chicken. Serve, if you like, with mashed potatoes made in the usual manner, but using olive oil instead of cream.

SERVES 4 TO 6

1 1/2 sticks (1/4 pound plus 4 tablespoons) butter,
*   at room temperature*
1 cup chopped fresh parsley
Salt and freshly ground black pepper, to taste
1 roasting chicken (about 4 pounds)
Juice of 1 lemon
2 tablespoons peanut oil or safflower oil
1 medium-sized carrot, cut into 5 pieces
1 onion, quartered

In a medium-sized bowl, whip together with a fork the butter, parsley, salt, and pepper to make a homogeneous mixture. Alternatively, this can be done in a blender or food processor. Chill the parsley butter several hours, but soften to room temperature again before using.

Preheat the oven to 400°F. With your fingers, carefully spread the parsley butter between the skin and the flesh of the bird over both the breasts and the thighs. This can be done without piercing the skin by wetting your hands and passing them under the neck flap of skin over the white meat. Fold back the skin to enclose the butter and fasten tightly closed with a skewer. Truss the chicken with kitchen twine, making several turns around the bird to keep the neck flap closed and the legs tightly together during cooking. The butter should remain imprisoned as much as possible.

Season the bird with salt and pepper and place it on its side in a roasting pan. Rub with 1 tablespoon each of lemon juice and peanut oil. Roast for 15 minutes in this position. Then turn onto the other side, rub again with 1 tablespoon each lemon juice and oil, and cook for another 15 minutes. Then add the carrot and onion to the pan, turn and place the chicken on its back to finish the cooking until the juices run clear when pierced at the leg joint with a fork, another 30 to 40 minutes. Sprinkle regularly with lemon juice throughout. If the bird gets too brown before being cooked through, cover with a sheet of aluminum foil.

Take the chicken out of the oven, and remove the string. Remove the carrot and onion pieces from the pan juices and adjust the seasoning with salt and pepper. Serve the juices in a separate bowl.

•

STRAWBERRY CRISPS WITH WHITE CHOCOLATE MOUSSE
Croustillant aux fraises et mousse au chocolat blanc

Escoffier also loved Provençal strawberries. In his *Fraises à la Sarah Bernhardt*, whole berries mingled with crushed ones, which had been simply macerated in sugar and brandy, then folded into whipped cream. Layered with fresh pineapple pulp and vanilla ice cream, this mixture produced the effect of a dazzling sunset, said the great chef, a worthy homage to a brilliant actress. Chenet's version is characteristically more discrete, but equally beautiful. It is a dessert of pure indulgence for chocolate lovers.
SERVES 4

33

WHITE CHOCOLATE MOUSSE

6 ounces best quality white chocolate,
  broken into bits
1 1/4 cup whipping cream, unsweetened and beaten
  until soft peaks form

CRISPS

2 cups roasted (page 155) and finely ground
  hazelnuts (8 to 10 ounces shelled nuts)
1 cup sugar
1 tablespoon all-purpose flour
3 tablespoons water
1/2 stick (4 tablespoons) butter, melted, plus
  more for cookie sheets

STRAWBERRIES

1 pint strawberries, hulled
3 tablespoons sugar or to taste
1 cup whipping cream with 2 tablespoons vanilla
  extract, beaten until soft peaks form

To Prepare the Mousse

Melt the chocolate in the top of a double boiler over barely simmering water until melted and glossy. Cool until nearly at room temperature but still liquid. Quickly and delicately fold chocolate into the whipped cream, pour into a large bowl, cover with plastic wrap, and chill.

To Prepare the Crisps

Preheat the oven to 350°F. In a medium-sized mixing bowl, combine the ground hazelnuts, sugar, and flour. Stir in the water and melted butter. On buttered cookie sheets, widely space 12 walnut-sized balls of dough. Bake until an even golden brown, about 10 minutes. Cool on the pans until just firm enough to remove with a metal spatula. Transfer to metal racks and let cool.

To Assemble the Dessert

In another bowl, mix the strawberries with the sugar. Purée 1/2 cup of the berries in a blender or food processor and set aside.

On each of 4 crisps, spread a layer of the whole strawberries, then spoon a layer of whipped cream over them. Repeat layers, alternating crisps, strawberries, and cream, ending with a crisp. Spoon a circle of the strawberry purée on each of 4 serving plates. Place on it a layered berry crisp. Using an ice-cream scoop, place balls of chocolate mousse next to each crisp.

Land of Legend

MENU

TRUFFLE AND POTATO SALAD
Salade de truffes fraîches aux pommes de terre

FILLETS OF SOLE WITH BABY SQUID, TOMATOES, AND SAFFRON
*Filets de sôle aux supions et aux pâtes
à l'encre noir*

SADDLE OF RABBIT WITH BASIL WINE SAUCE
Rable de lapin au basilic

HOT PISTACHIO SOUFFLÉ
Soufflé chaud à la pistache

JEAN-ANDRÉ CHARIAL   *Oustau de Baumanière*   LES-BAUX-DE-PROVENCE

The village of Les-Baux-de-Provence rises in the heart of the Alpilles mountains, described by poet Frédéric Mistral as "a range of rocky Greek crags, looking down on a land of glorious deeds and legends." This striking site has lent itself to romance since medieval times, when the counts of Les Baux claimed descendance from Balthazar, one of the biblical three kings of the Magi. The star still appears on the coat of arms of the town. "A comet race" they were, according to English writer James Pope-Hennessey, "baleful to the neighboring lowlands, blazing with lurid splendour." One fourteenth-century descendant gained fame as a terrifying outlaw, whose prisoners were forced to jump from his castle's high battlements. But this same ruffian's ward, Alix des Baux, became a symbol of refinement and civilization, presiding over a brilliant court which applauded troubadours and set the codes of behavior for courtly love. Today the title of Marquis des Baux belongs to a much more peaceable lord: the eldest son of Prince Ranier of Monaco, who has on occasion been received in state by the townspeople.

Land of legend indeed. But today's mythmakers concentrate on the new lords of Les Baux, owners and chefs of the Oustau de Baumanière, a world-renowned establishment which first opened its doors for Christmas, 1945. Its founding father was Raymond Thuilier, a former insurance salesman who had the forethought to restore a picturesque olive oil mill at the foot of the cliffs of Les Baux during the German occupation in World War II. His sole professional experience in food had been growing up around his mother's small restaurant. Already fifty-one years old at the end of the war, active

JEAN-ANDRÉ CHARIAL

in politics and a painter of some renown, Thuilier succeeded so well in his new venture that he achieved three Michelin stars in less than ten years.

Thus began the Baumanière legend. The entire community was to feel its effects. Before Baumanière, the town lay neglected and abandoned, inspiring generation after generation of ninteenth-century visitors to describe its eerie effect: For composer Charles-François Gounod, Les Baux was "a marvel of savagery"; for Henry James, "a mere confusion of ruins"; for British scholar John Addington Symonds, the town was "like a decayed old cheese." Southern novelist Alphonse Daudet movingly made the gutted houses of Les Baux a symbol of the declining Provençal language. And Prosper Mérimée noted a mail box on one ruined wall in 1834 and wondered, who would ever write a letter to Les Baux?

The same wall today may be hung with a rack of postcards. In any case, it has certainly been restored, along with the rest of this particularly picturesque hill town— all thanks to the success of the Oustau de Baumanière and the efforts of Raymond Thuilier, who was mayor of Les Baux for decades.

The surrounding countryside remains unchanged, haunting and as romantic as ever. To the north can be seen the tortured cliffs of the Valley of Hell. Here bauxite was discovered in 1822, and from the village perched above, the angular openings of old quarries add to the geometries of an already lunar landscape. Indeed, the northern approach to Les Baux has such weird and tortured rock formations (many thought to resemble witches' faces with hooked noses) that it is said to have inspired Dante for the landscapes of his *Inferno*. Jean Cocteau used the setting to shoot his film *Orpheus*.

Cocteau, of course, ate at Baumanière and has left a drawing and his greetings to the chef on the menu's cover. He was but one of the celebrities to help create the legend of Baumanière. The Queen of England deigned to eat there in 1972. In the 1980s, a cartoon in *The New Yorker* depicted a husband and wife preparing dinner together, he at the stove and she washing the salad. The caption read: "One wonders what they're serving tonight at Oustau de Baumanière in Les Baux." People all over the world still ask the question today.

Raymond Thuilier remained lord of Les Baux for over forty years, a grand old patriarch of French gastronomy. Few figures better exemplify Escoffier's image of the chef de cuisine as an artist to be revered, rather than merely a cook, a servant among servants. Long before chefs became the media stars that many are today, Thuilier imposed respect for his newly adopted profession. He died in 1993, older than the century.

The prince of Les Baux today is Jean-André Charial, one of Thuilier's grandsons who left a budding engineering career to become heir to the throne. Grandfather Thuilier was a hard taskmaster, as becomes a patriarch of the old school, and Charial underwent a rigorous apprenticeship. After working with many of the great names of the time (the Troisgros brothers, Bernard Loiseau, Alain Chapel, Paul and Marc Haeberlin), he took over the kitchen of Baumanière in the early 1970s. Thuilier continued to be present at every service until 1992.

During these twenty years, the Oustau de Baumanière has grown into a small empire. Further down the valley, the initial establishment is seconded by La Cabro d'Oro, a more modest hotel and restaurant where Charial nonetheless supervises and plans the food service, and now there is a branch in London as well, the Auberge de Provence.

Although the Alpilles region is one of the great producers of choice fruit and vegetables (the wholesale market of Saint-Etienne-du-Grès is only a few miles away), Baumanière continues to cultivate its own orchards and vegetable gardens at Les Baux and Maussane. Thus chef Charial can serve very tiny green beans, for example, or aromatics not commonly found in Provence such as dill and coriander. There are now shops selling

Baumanière products (herbs, mustards, teas and coffees, wine, alcohols, jams, olive oil, sachets), and there have been three cookbooks. Just recently the restaurant has become partner in the beautiful caves of the Château de Romanin (Côteaux d'Aix). And there are cooking courses on Saturday mornings, mostly frequented by local people. Jean-André Charial oversees all of this with careful attention.

In the kitchen, he is seconded by Alain Burnel, himself a Maître Cuisinier de France. In summer there are twenty people working here, all highly professional, no temporary help. To be apprenticed at Baumanière is a great asset in any young chef's career. What does the kitchen look like going full strength? Writer Frédéric Dard compares it to a rocket launching at NASA or an operating room during a heart transplant. Everyone displays

intense concentration; all movement is the rigorous result of years of training.

Like all great legends, Baumanière has its detractors. The third Michelin star was lost in 1989. Was this because food critics questioned whether titles should be handed down from generation to generation in gastronomic as in aristrocratic families? Charial has had to work extra hard to prove that he deserved his inheritance. He has been told, moreover, that he is not *gracieux*, a Provençal term meaning sociable or approachable. And yet his friend Dard says that Charial has found his own style, less expansive perhaps than Thuilier's, but that of an "attentive gentleman . . . proud of what he loves."

Everyone comes to Baumanière. At the same time, Charial travels extensively, participating in gastronomic festivities and manifestations all over the world. He considers that his cuisine is cosmopolitan, open to outside influences: So it is that a trip to Morocco some years ago inspired a dish of honeyed pigeon. But such experimentation is possible, he feels, because he remains rooted in the *terroir* that is Provence. His cooking is always based on olive oil (from the famous mill at nearby Maussane), though he uses butter and cream to enrich sauces. In spite of his heavy administrative responsibilities, he much prefers the creative side of his profession to management.

Neither technique nor presentation interest Charial so much as original associations—as in his smooth, sweet-pepper soup with clams and ginger. The following menu shows clearly his enjoyment of cuisine as a delight for all the senses at once. Even a sauce, he says, must be tasted with the fingers and judged by look and smell, as well as the palate. The fish recipe with a saffron sauce provides an excellent opportunity to follow the chef's example!

•

Truffle and Potato Salad
Salade de truffes fraîches aux pommes de terre

Contrast of texture, temperature, and color all play important roles in this blend of truffles and hot fried potatoes served on mixed greens. Charial prefers the French Ratte variety of potato, which has firm, yellow flesh and good flavor.
Serves 4

3 ounces truffles
Juice of 1/2 lemon
Salt and freshly ground black pepper, to taste
7 tablespoons extra-virgin olive oil
3 tablespoons sherry vinegar
2 medium-sized potatoes (preferably yellow-fleshed), peeled
2 tablespoons butter
3 cups mixed salad greens (mâche, red chicory, arugula, curly endive)

Cut 2 1/2 ounces of the truffles into thin rounds and finely chop the remainder. In a small bowl, mix the lemon juice, salt, and pepper. Add the minced truffles and beat in 4 tablespoons of the olive oil with a fork to make a vinaigrette dressing.

In another small bowl, make a second dressing with the sherry vinegar, salt, pepper, and remaining 3 tablespoons of olive oil.

Cut the potatoes into thin rounds. Heat the butter to medium high in a small skillet and sauté the potatoes, turning often, until crisp and cooked through, about 15 minutes.

In a large bowl, toss the greens with the sherry vinegar dressing and arrange on 4 plates. Arrange the truffle slices on top in a circle, and spoon over the truffle vinaigrette. Top with the hot, fried potato rounds and serve immediately.

•

Fillets of Sole with Baby Squid, Tomatoes, and Saffron
Filets de sôle aux supions et aux pâtes à l'encre noir

Cuttlefish are small squid, about two inches long, with large "ears." But any type of squid could be used as long as it is not too tough. Ask your fishmonger to remove the blade and ink sack, as this is tricky to do at home. Black pasta, made with squid ink, makes a particularly stunning contrast with the saffron sauce and the tomato garnish. To order black pasta by mail, see the list of suppliers on page 153. Any fettuccine-type pasta could be substituted, however, including the green spinach variety. At Baumanière, small soles are used in this dish; whole white fish such as plaice, rex sole, or sand dabs would be suitable. Ask your fishmonger for some fish bones to make the stock.
Serves 4

3/4 pound small cuttlefish, cleaned, or any small squid
2 tablespoons olive oil
1 cup fish stock (page 155) or bottled clam juice
1 cup dry white wine
2 shallots, minced
1/2 teaspoon tomato paste
Butter, for greasing pan
4 small, whole white fish (about 12 ounces each),
  cleaned and scaled
2 cups crème fraîche or heavy cream
Pinch of saffron
Salt and freshly ground black pepper, to taste
10 ounces dried squid-ink pasta or spinach fettuccine
1 ripe tomato, peeled, seeded, and diced, for garnish

Preheat the oven to 450°F. Cut the cuttlefish into fine strips, wash and dry them. In a medium-sized skillet, heat the olive oil over high heat, and sauté the cuttlefish strips until lightly colored, 3 to 4 minutes. Add 1/2 cup of the fish stock, 1/2 cup of the white wine, I of the minced shallots, and the tomato paste. Reduce the heat and simmer until tender, about 20 minutes. Drain and reserve the juice, keeping the cuttlefish warm.

Butter a shallow flameproof roasting pan or an ovenproof skillet just large enough to hold the whole fishes. Lay the fish in the pan and spoon over the remaining 1/2 cup white wine and the remaining 1/2 cup fish stock. Sprinkle with the remaining minced shallot. Bake in hot oven until just cooked through, about 10 minutes.

Remove the fish from the pan. Fillet them, remove bones, and keep warm on a serving dish. Add the reserved cuttlefish juices, crème fraîche, and saffron to the cooking juices in the pan, scraping the bottom to mix. Put the pan on a burner over medium heat, and boil down the sauce until it is thickened, about 10 minutes. Adjust the seasoning with salt and pepper.

While the sauce is reducing, bring to a boil a large saucepan of salted water and cook the pasta al dente.

On each of 4 plates, arrange the pasta in the center and the fish fillets around the outside, alternating with the cuttlefish. Spoon the sauce over all in a decorative manner. Put a tablespoon of diced tomato on each plate. Serve immediately.

•

SADDLE OF RABBIT WITH BASIL WINE SAUCE
Rable de lapin au basilic

The wild hills around Les Baux are full of rabbits, who feed on the thyme and savory that grows in the crevices of these rocks. This dish could easily be made with chicken breasts, however, and it could also be made using all the pieces of one medium-sized rabbit.
SERVES 4

2 saddles of rabbit (about 12 ounces each) or
  1 whole rabbit (3 to 4 pounds), cut into 4 pieces
6 tablespoons chopped fresh basil
Salt and freshly ground pepper, to taste
2 tablespoons olive oil
12 cloves garlic, unpeeled
8 shallots, minced
1 cup dry white wine
1/4 cup chicken broth or stock (store-bought or page 155)
1/2 stick (4 tablespoons) butter, cut up

Preheat the oven to 400°F. Make a long slit on either side of the bone in each rabbit saddle or piece. Insert I tablespoon of the chopped basil in each slit. Season the meat with salt and pepper. In a medium-sized skillet that can also go into the oven or a flameproof casserole, heat the olive oil over medium-high heat and add the rabbit, garlic, and shallots. Turn the meat so that it browns evenly, 3 to 4 minutes.

42

Place the pan in the hot oven and cook 10 to 15 minutes more, taking care that the meat does not overcook. In France, rabbit saddles are eaten quite rare, but a whole rabbit would require longer cooking, 20 to 30 minutes.

Remove meat from the pan with a slotted spoon, transfer to a plate and keep it warm. Add the wine to the cooking juices, scraping up bits from the bottom of the pan. Add the chicken stock and blend well. Strain the juices into a small bowl and add the remaining 2 tablespoons basil. Beat in the butter to thicken the sauce and adjust the seasoning. Return the sauce to the pan and reheat without boiling.

Arrange the meat on a serving plate and spoon the sauce over it. Serve immediately.

•

HOT PISTACHIO SOUFFLÉ
Soufflé chaud à la pistache

Pistachios grow on the Riviera although not in inland Provence. More luxurious than almonds for that reason, these nuts were traditionally used in the Provençal baking as extra enrichment, in the honey nougat, for example, eaten at Christmas time. Pistachio paste is a ready-made preparation of roasted, finely ground nuts mixed with sugar. If it is hard to find, the much more common almond paste could be used in the soufflé, and chopped pistachios in the sauce.

SERVES 4

1 1/2 cups sugar syrup (page 155)
1 1/2 cups roughly chopped, blanched almonds
2 1/2 cups milk
4 egg yolks
1/2 cup granulated white sugar
1 1/2 tablespoons all-purpose flour
3 ounces pistachio paste or almond paste
6 egg whites
Butter and powdered sugar, for soufflé dishes
1 tablespoon chopped pistachios
1 tablespoon chopped, roasted hazelnuts (page 155)

Put the sugar syrup into a medium-sized saucepan and bring slowly to a boil. Remove from the heat, fold in the almonds, and let sit, covered, for 2 hours. Pour into a blender or food processor and blend into a smooth sauce. Strain through a fine sieve into a bowl and set aside.

Preheat the oven to 450°F. Scald the milk in the top of a double boiler over simmering water. In a large bowl, beat the egg yolks until lemon colored, sprinkle the sugar and the flour over them, and blend well. Slowly pour in the scalded milk, stirring all the time, then return the mixture to the double boiler. Cook, stirring over low heat until the custard thickens. Strain into a large bowl. Divide the pistachio paste into small bits and gently whisk into the custard while it is still hot. Set aside to cool.

In another large bowl, beat the egg whites until firm. Fold into the cooled custard mixture. Butter 4 individual 2-cup soufflé dishes (4 1/2 x 2 inches) and sprinkle with powdered sugar. Divide half the custard mixture among the 4 dishes, sprinkle with the chopped pistachios and hazelnuts, then fill with the remaining custard.

Place the soufflé dishes on a baking sheet for easy handling and bake until golden, about 15 minutes. Make a slit in the top of each soufflé and pour in a little of the sauce. Serve immediately with the rest of the almond sauce separately.

Summer Lunch on the Terrace

MENU

SUMMER VEGETABLE SALAD WITH BASIL
Légumes d'été aux senteurs de basilic

UPSIDE-DOWN CHICKEN PIE WITH TAPENADE
Tarte à l'envers de volaille à la tapenade

SPICED MONKFISH IN PHYLLO PASTRY
Croustillon de lotte aux épices, en feuille de brick

ELISABETH'S CHEESE TERRINE
Le Parfait fromagé d'Elisabeth

CHILLED RED FRUITS IN MINT SYRUP
Ma soupe de quatre fruits

ELISABETH BOURGEOIS   *Le Mas Tourteron*   GORDES

Every summer, the hill towns of Provence fill up with vacationers and visitors of every description. But few of these spots have achieved the international acclaim of Gordes. All visitors find their way through the maze of tiny streets into the large market square by the massive Renaissance château, transformed by op artist Vasarély into a museum of his work. Novelist André Brink, in *The Wall of the Plague*, imagined his heroine admiring Gordes' "alluring little shops: the silversmiths, the joiner, the candlemakers, the honey vendors, the potters, the sellers of small jars of citronella or lavender to keep away mosquitoes, the weavers . . ."

But this town is much more than the frequently photographed golden triangle of its perched village, where summer throngs can become cloying in the heat. Luckily,

Gordes' territory extends broadly over the surrounding hills, looking down on the Calavon river as it snakes along the valley, among patchwork fields, towards Apt. Gordes includes numerous outlying hamlets, winding country roads and lanes, and those curious dry-stone huts called *bories*, whose domes pepper the landscape and mystify historians and archeologists. Here and there are sprawling farmsteads locally known by the name of *mas*.

The heroine of Brink's novel also sought seclusion after her encounter with the town market. She drove down from the village along country roads fragrant with wild-growing herbs, past vineyards and olive orchards, and "bare fields where lavender and wheat had lain so unashamedly in the sun . . ." On that occasion she ended up discovering an old farmhouse restaurant built of "honey-coloured stone" with a "terracotta roof and tall cypresses." Here she and her companion enjoyed "an incomparable meal on the terrace."

Today she would almost certainly be describing Le Mas Tourteron. Elisabeth Bourgeois and her husband Phillipe Baique have transformed this picturesque building into an oasis of pleasure hidden among the fields and vineyards of the open countryside. A *borie* built into the north wall now shelters the wine cellar. Facing south, as is traditional for rural dwellings in Provence, the farmhouse looks onto the valley and the great blue whale of the Luberon ridge rising against the far horizon.

The courtyard behind the stone gate has become a quiet garden terrace for shaded summer dining. In the vast dining room, various collections cluster around the carved wooden fireplace or on discrete side tables: miniature stoves complete in every detail, bird cages, farm tools, coffee mills. Colorful bouquets of dry and fresh flowers, arranged by the cook herself, show the same creativity with simple country materials evident in her cuisine. Madame Bourgeois has given her farmstead the air of a private residence, arranged with the taste of the best (and most famous) antiques dealers of nearby Isle-sur-la-Sorgue, that international mecca for country décor. The china is made at the factory in Gien, exclusively for her restaurant.

The same meticulous attention to detail is evident in the kitchen, visible behind the reception desk on entering—an efficient but esthetic arrangement centering on the huge, black Moréni stove. Here a team of four young women work under the vigilant eye of *la patronne*, while Phillipe Baique, Madame Bourgeois' husband, acts as both wine steward and receptionist. About sixty people can be served here at a time, though in summer, with the outdoor terrace, the number can reach one hundred.

Le Mas Tourteron has been open since 1978. Needless to say, Madame Bourgeois' career has not been the same as those of her male colleagues. Winner of the trophy of *Mères cuisinières*, she acknowledges her descendance from that great tradition of gastronomic "mothers" who ran restaurants, especially around Lyons, and who influenced so many of the great contemporary chefs. She often provides menus and recipes for leading French women's magazines. But she feels that *la cuisine des femmes* can also limit young women today who simply wish to become great cooks on the open market, not in a special category of family style. Female chefs today can be found at the bottom and at the top of the professional ladder, she observes, but rarely in the middle. Elisabeth Bourgeois wishes to be known, like her male colleagues (who speak very highly of her), for her artistry and her professionalism—and little by little, this wish is being granted.

At Le Mas Tourteron, sophisticated country décor provides enjoyment for the eye, and country savors supply equivalent pleasures for the palate. Particularly innovative with vegetables, Madame Bourgeois experiments with the dense, red squash beloved by organic gardeners, the *potimarron* with its echoes of chestnut flavor. She makes an old-fashioned *tian du jardinier provençal*, the southern baked vegetable dish, as well as the traditional zucchini,

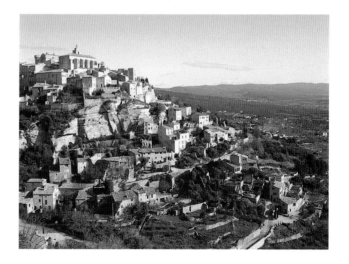

ELISABETH BOURGEOIS

tomatoes, and peppers with a *farandole* of different stuffings. The classic Provençal *papeton*, in which an eggplant-lined mold was filled with lamb, has become in her inventive hands a subtly spiced lamb charlotte. Asian influences creep in: The summer menu features spring rolls of fresh tuna with tomato fritters and sage butter; and in autumn there is a laquered breast of partridge with tiny ravioli, sprinkled with sesame seeds. For those who like old-fashioned country fare, there is a cabbage stuffed with wild rabbit and lambs' feet. The secret of this dish's richly perfumed sauce is ground wild mushrooms.

The recipes that follow are all simple to prepare, highly original, and even witty elaborations of old country themes. This is the ideal, hot-weather menu, accompanied by the singing of cicadas in the sear grass all around this privileged oasis.

SUMMER VEGETABLE SALAD WITH BASIL
Légumes d'été aux senteurs de basilic

A lovely medley of the best Provençal vegetables of the season, served with a poached, farm-fresh egg to enrich the sauce. If you're concerned about the risk of salmonella being in soft-cooked eggs, buy pasteurized eggs for this dish or omit altogether. The salad tastes best if all the vegetables are lukewarm when it is served.
SERVES 4

Salt, as needed
1 pound green asparagus, trimmed and peeled
1 pound baby carrots with their leaves
3 medium-sized artichokes
2 tablespoons fresh lemon juice
1/4 pound fava beans, shelled and peeled
1/4 pound snow peas, trimmed and cut in half lengthwise
1 tablespoon balsamic vinegar
4 eggs
Freshly ground black pepper, to taste
1/4 cup olive oil
4 tablespoons chopped fresh basil
1 tablespoon pine nuts

Bring a large saucepan of salted water to a boil. Add the asparagus and simmer until just tender, about 5 minutes. Remove the asparagus from the saucepan with a slotted spoon and dip quickly into a bowl of ice water. Drain immediately and reserve.

Bring the water in the saucepan to a boil once more. Cut back the carrot leaves to ³/4-inch lengths. Boil the carrots until just barely cooked, about 5 minutes. Dip into ice water, drain, and reserve.

Remove the outer leaves and stems from the artichokes. Cut them in quarters, remove the chokes, and rub them with lemon juice. Bring the water in the saucepan to a boil once again, put in the artichokes and boil until just tender, about 5 minutes. Remove with a slotted spoon, dip into ice water, drain, and reserve.

Bring the water in the saucepan to a boil once more. Put in the fava beans and cook until tender, about 3 minutes. Remove with a slotted spoon, dip into ice water, drain, and reserve. Repeat the operation with the snow peas, cooking for about 2 minutes. Rinse, drain, and reserve.

Put about 1 inch of salted water in a medium-sized skillet and heat to a simmer. Add a few drops of vinegar. Poach the eggs in the skillet until the yolks are just beginning to get firm, about 5 minutes. Line a plate with paper towels. Transfer the eggs to the plate with a slotted spoon.

To prepare the dressing, put the remaining vinegar in a bowl and beat in salt and pepper with a fork, then beat in the olive oil and 2 tablespoons of the chopped basil.

To serve, arrange the carrots, fava beans, snow peas, and artichoke quarters on each of 4 plates. Divide the asparagus among the plates, arranging them side by side to form a bed for the poached egg. Place 1 egg on each bed of asparagus. (Their yolks should run over the asparagus tips when broken.) Decorate with the pine nuts and remaining 2 tablespoons basil. Spoon over the dressing and serve lukewarm.

•

UPSIDE-DOWN CHICKEN PIE
WITH TAPENADE
Tarte à l'envers de volaille à la tapenade

The ideal dish for lunch on the terrace, quintessentially Provençal but with an original flourish. Madame Bourgeois often makes this pie with young rabbit (*lapereau*). Tapenade is a paste of black olives, sometimes enriched with capers and anchovies, which can be purchased in small jars at specialty shops (see page 153 for sources) or made at home. Pascal Morel's recipe for Rolled Sole Fillets (page 93) offers one version.
SERVES 4

7 ripe but firm tomatoes (about 1 pound)
6 to 10 tablespoons olive oil
3 shallots, minced
1 clove garlic, crushed
1 sprig fresh thyme
1 tablespoon finely chopped fresh basil
Salt and freshly ground black pepper, to taste
3/4 cup tapenade (store-bought or page 93)
4 boneless chicken breast halves (about 2 pounds
    total), skinned
4 long, thin eggplants, peeled and cut lengthwise
    into thin slices
12 ounces puff pastry (store-bought or page 153)
2 chicken livers
4 sprigs fresh basil or parsley, for garnish

Preheat the oven to 350°F. Peel and dice 3 of the tomatoes. Heat 1/2 tablespoon of the olive oil in a small skillet over medium heat. Add the diced tomatoes, 1 minced shallot, the garlic, thyme, chopped basil, salt, and pepper. Simmer until thick, 10 to 15 minutes. Remove from the heat and cool. Mix in the tapenade.

Heat 2 tablespoons of the olive oil in a large skillet over medium-high heat. Add the chicken breasts and cook until brown, turning once, about 5 minutes on each side. Add the remaining minced shallots after turning. The meat should be just golden but still raw inside, and the shallots lightly browned. Remove shallots and chicken from the pan onto a plate. Cut the chicken into 9 or 10 neat slices and reserve all.

Heat 2 more tablespoons of the olive oil in the same skillet and brown the eggplant slices on both sides, adding more oil if necessary during cooking. Remove the

slices with a slotted spoon as they brown and let them drain on paper towels. Sprinkle with salt and pepper. Cut the 4 remaining tomatoes into thin rounds.

To assemble the pie, oil a nonstick, 9-inch cake pan. Arrange in a pretty pattern a layer of raw tomato and eggplant slices, then the chicken breasts. Cover with a fine layer of the cooked tomato and tapenade mixture.

Roll out the pastry into a circle slightly larger than the diameter of the pan and spread over the top. Tuck in the edges. Prick the pastry with a fork and chill the pie 10 minutes.

Bake the pie until nicely browned, about 20 minutes. Remove it from the oven and unmold it carefully onto a large serving plate, with the pastry on the bottom.

While the pie is baking, heat 1 tablespoon of the olive oil in a small skillet. Cook the whole chicken livers over medium heat until browned but still pink inside, about 3 minutes. Cut them into fine slices. Arrange the sliced livers with the fresh basil or parsley sprigs in the center of the pie just before serving.

•

SPICED MONKFISH IN PHYLLO PASTRY
Croustillon de lotte aux épices, en feuille de brick

This is an intriguing dish with obvious Moroccan influences. Elisabeth Bourgeois' use of pastry to provide unusual but efficient envelopes for different savory mixtures is particularly inventive. Pickled lemon can be found in Middle Eastern specialty shops. Alternatively, lemon slices can be placed in a small saucepan, just barely

covered with a mixture of two parts salted water to one part olive oil, and simmered until soft. Frozen phyllo dough can be found at better supermarkets or Middle Eastern groceries and must be defrosted overnight in the refrigerator. In this recipe, Bourgeois uses *lotte* (the Atlantic anglerfish or monkfish), but any firm white fish will do. Accompany this with a salad of mixed greens.
SERVES 4

3 tablespoons olive oil
1 onion, minced
1 red pepper and 1 green bell pepper, roasted and
  seeded (page 155) and cut into thin strips
2 ripe, medium-sized tomatoes, peeled, seeded, and diced
1 small hot green chili pepper, seeded and minced
1 clove garlic, crushed
1 tablespoon ground ginger
Salt and freshly ground black pepper, to taste
2 tablespoons chopped fresh coriander (cilantro)
4 leaves phyllo dough, thawed overnight in refrigerator
4 slices (about 1/4 inch thick) pickled lemon
  (see above)
4 anglerfish steaks (about 1 1/3 pounds total), cut
  from the tail end if possible, about 1/2 inch thick
  and 3 inches wide
1 bunch chives, for garnish

Preheat the oven to 325°F. Heat 2 tablespoons of the olive oil in a medium-sized skillet over medium heat and cook the onion, red and green pepper strips, and tomatoes for 5 minutes. Stir in the minced hot pepper, garlic, ginger, salt, and pepper. Cook over low heat until soft, about 10 minutes. Remove from the heat and mix in the coriander.

Grease four 5-inch gratin dishes with the remaining olive oil, and spread 1 sheet of phyllo dough in each dish, with the edges hanging over the sides. Place on top

of each phyllo sheet a slice of pickled lemon and top each with 1 slice of fish. Spoon over this the cooked vegetables, dividing them evenly among the molds. Now fold the 4 corners of each phyllo sheet over the filling, twisting lightly so the "bags" will remain closed during baking. It is not necessary to brush the dough with any fat.

Place the gratin dishes on a baking sheet and bake until golden brown, about 12 minutes. The pastry will be dry and crispy on top, the filling moist and savory. Place two chives, crisscrossed, on each *croustillon* before serving, to look like string. Serve very hot.

•

ELISABETH'S CHEESE TERRINE
Le Parfait fromagé d'Elisabeth

This dish recalls the blended cheese logs that American cuisine, with its love of mixtures, has long appreciated. In France this concept is still close to heresy. Madame Bourgeois pulls it off with panache.
SERVES 4

5 sticks (1 1/4 pounds) unsalted butter,
  at room temperature
1/4 cup anchovy fillets in oil, drained
Freshly ground black pepper, to taste
3/4 pound Roquefort cheese, at room
  temperature, crumbled
3 tablespoons finely chopped fresh chives
1 teaspoon peanut oil or safflower oil
3 to 4 ounces Comté or Gruyère cheese, thinly sliced
2 tablespoons finely ground hazelnuts
2 tablespoons finely ground almonds
1 bunch sorrel, large stems discarded
Salad of mixed greens, for garnish, dressed
  with vinaigrette

ELISABETH BOURGEOIS

Chill a small, rectangular glass, ceramic, or metal terrine or loaf pan (roughly 6x2¹/₂x3 inches).

In a blender or food processor or with a whisk, combine 2 sticks of the butter with the anchovies, and season with pepper. Transfer to a small bowl and set aside. Likewise combine the remaining butter with the Roquefort and chives. Set aside.

Remove the terrine from the refrigerator, brush it with the peanut oil, and line it with plastic wrap, leaving some to hang over the ends and sides. Line the bottom and sides of the mold with the thinly sliced Comté cheese. Using a rubber spatula, spread an even, ³/₄-inch layer of the Roquefort butter over the cheese slices in the bottom. Mix together the ground hazelnuts and almonds and sprinkle ¹/₃ over the Roquefort layer. Next, spread over a few sorrel leaves, then a very thin layer of the anchovy butter, and more Gruyère. Repeat the same sequence a second time, again finishing with the Gruyère. Fold over the plastic wrap to close and refrigerate for 1 hour. Press down lightly on the top with a spatula to solidify the mixture. Return to refrigerator for another hour.

To serve, arrange a bed of the salad greens on each

of 4 serving plates. Divide the terrine into 8 even slices, each about ³/₄ inch thick. Remove carefully from the dish, pulling off the plastic wrap, and place 2 slices on top of the greens on each plate. Sprinkle with the remaining ground nuts and serve.

•

CHILLED RED FRUITS
IN MINT SYRUP
Ma soupe de quatre fruits

This is a fresh, midsummer soup, simple to prepare (with minimal cooking) and very flavorful.
SERVES 4

2 cups water
2 cups sugar
2 pints strawberries, hulled
1 tablespoon plus ¹/₃ cup fresh lemon juice
¹/₂ pound cherries, stoned
¹/₂ pound raspberries
¹/₂ pound red currants
Leaves from 1 bunch fresh mint, cut finely with scissors

Put the water into a medium-sized saucepan, add the sugar, and stir constantly over low heat until the sugar dissolves. Bring the mixture to a strong boil, then reduce heat and simmer for 15 minutes without stirring. Remove from heat and leave to cool.

With a food processor or blender, purée half the strawberries with 1 cup of the sugar syrup and 1 tablespoon lemon juice. Set aside. Halve the remaining strawberries.

In a large, pretty serving bowl, put the remaining syrup, then the puréed strawberries. Arrange in layers on top the cherries, raspberries, red currants, and the halved strawberries. Sprinkle with ¹/₃ cup lemon juice and the mint slivers. Chill for 2 hours before serving.

Christmas Cuisine from the Ventoux

MENU

CELERY ROOT AND TRUFFLE GRATIN
WITH CURLY ENDIVE SALAD
Gratin de céléris aux truffes fraîches en vinaigrette

OLIVE-STUFFED FISH ROUNDS
Rouelles de mulet farcies aux olives de Nyons

WINTER WHEAT AND SAUTÉED SPINACH
Risotto d'épeautre et poelée d'épinards

THE THIRTEEN DESSERTS OF CHRISTMAS—
QUINCE DUMPLINGS
Les "Treize Desserts" avec les coings entiers cuits au four

PHILIPPE MONTI   *Hostellerie de Crillon-le-Brave*   CRILLON-LE-BRAVE (MALAUCÈNE)

The white cone of Mont Ventoux, rising some six thousand feet above fields and vineyards, dominates the entire countryside northeast of Avignon. Its name derives from the Celtic word for wind. Its barren top (white limestone which looks snowy even in summer) is now accessible by car and offers one of the most stunning panoramas of the region.

For centuries, its ascent was perilous: Only shepherds seeking lost sheep ventured up its slopes. The first climber to climb to the top out of curiosity was the great poet and humanist Petrarch, in 1336. Other daring souls explored the mountain in the spirit of scientific inquiry about once every hundred years until the nineteenth century. Then the naturalist, Jean-Henri Fabre, went up more than twenty-five times, studying vegetation which still ranges from African to arctic. During his lifetime, the mountain's eroded middle slopes underwent intensive reforestation, so that today they are dark with majestic pines and cedars.

The Ventoux now combines spectacular, unspoiled landscapes with some of the most charming—and little known—villages of Provence. Nature lovers still find its slopes a particularly rich hunting ground but must beware of gun-toting hunters in the autumn! Hikers, climbers, bicyclists, and skiers haunt the mountain, each in the appropriate season. Bird-watchers can find here the majestic Bonelli's eagle (poet René Char described this mountain as an "eagles' mirror"). Photographers get excited about sheets of lavender or patterned cherry orchards. Wheat was once grown much more widely on these slopes, and many villages still have famous bakeries. Today the winter wheat known as *épeautre* has become a favorite of Provençal chefs who use it in most imaginative ways. But perhaps the king of the Ventoux is the truffle. The Friday morning market in Carpentras, on the plain south of the mountain, is famous in winter for its hard bargaining for these black diamonds.

One of the most charming villages of the Ventoux's

rolling foothills is Crillon-le-Brave, near Malaucène, named for a sixteenth-century soldier whose statue presides in the heart of town. In Crillon, as in all of the mountain villages, an old church and castle stand dramatically silhouetted against the surrounding valley. Here the white peak of the Ventoux rises to the northeast of town.

Crillon's castle has been converted into the hotel and restaurant Hostellerie de Crillon-le-Brave by Canadian businessman Peter Chittick and his partner, Craig Miller. The twenty rooms of the hotel meet one's every expectation for both the comfort and the charms of a French country inn. Peter Chittick, with no professional training in the business, took great risks to promote a project about which he was passionately enthusiastic. The mayor of Crillon has been his fervent supporter.

The Hostellerie has become for many of its regular customers a home away from home; indeed its ocher-washed sitting rooms with their fireplaces and antique furniture, its library where chamber music concerts are held, are designed to create just that feeling of an elegant family residence rather than a hotel. It is a wonderful place to spend Christmas, cozily by the fire, or outdoors, walking or skiing in the bracing mountain air. The folklore of Provence has survived nowhere better than in these mountain villages, which still present miracle plays and carol singing in the old style.

Chef Monti is an artist who loves to experiment. His cuisine inevitably takes its inspiration from the wide range of products available in the area. Red mullet fillets are served simply with garlic and parsley juice. Local lamb is larded with truffles and served with a pumpkin purée. A mousse of dried apricots incorporates pine nuts. And fruit appears also with fish, such as monkfish tournedos with a quince coulis. The associations are often strikingly original: lamb cutlets with a cypress-flavored gratin, or a salmon tart with green onions and sea urchin butter. A tart of white peaches comes with tomato jam, a

casserole of summer figs simmers in a red wine and cinnamon sauce, and watermelon is served with a sherbet made from lime blossoms. Menus are changed three times a year for spring, summer, and autumn, when group cooking seminars are also held. But the Hostellerie de Crillon-le-Brave reopens in December for the full celebration of Provençal Christmas holiday customs.

Christmas in Provence is the most festive moment of the entire year. As with all Provençal festivals, Christmas traditions derive both from Roman Catholic ritual and from more ancient, pagan roots. In the Ventoux, as elsewhere in Provence, preparations begin on December 4, Saint Barbara's Day, when young children sow seeds of lentils, wheat, barley, or chickpeas in a saucer of water. Soon, the shallow dish will hold fresh shoots that will provide a lush touch of green for the *gros souper* or great supper of Christmas Eve, echoing a ritual that millenia ago paid homage to the Greek god Adonis.

During Advent, a Christmas crèche is set up on each family's table, using the handcrafted *santons* or dolls, representing local characters, like the garlic seller or the shepherd. It is as if Christ had been born in a Provençal village. A centuries-old tradition of depicting the nativity scene survives in the *pastourale* plays that villagers on the Mont Ventoux still perform throughout the holiday season.

Christmas Eve is the main focus of festivities, however, in Crillon as all over the region. A fruit tree that has died during the year must be cut down and brought back home in a joyful procession to serve as a yule log. Christmas coincides with the olive oil harvest, and an olive branch is used for the most important moment of the ceremony: Together, the oldest and youngest members of the family dip it in mulled wine, then anoint the yule log while saying in unison the following chant:

God give us joy, God give us joy,
Christmas is coming,
May God's grace ensure, in the coming year
That if we are not more, we may not be fewer.

This celebration is called the *Cacho-fio* and is the high point of Provençal Christmas ritual, linking as it does human growth and that of the land in prayer. A ceremonial bowl of mulled wine is then passed round.

Next comes the great banquet, the *gros souper*. This meal is lean (like Lent; meat and fat will be reintroduced on Christmas day). Nonetheless, this grand supper displays all the household's rich resources, fresh and preserved: Winter vegetables like cardoons, celery, and spinach are customarily served with fish and snails; cauliflower sown in April past (like a memory of spring fulfilled) may appear with anchovy sauce; a wonderfully fragrant fish stew with wine and capers is often served, and perhaps a capon flamed in Cognac. The banquet traditionally ends with the famous thirteen desserts (see notes on following recipe).

Certain villages, such as Séguret, near Crillon, still celebrate the old-fashioned midnight mass in Provençal which follows the *gros souper*. Here shepherds present a Christmas lamb at the altar as an offering. The animal is carried in a cart decorated with fruit and flowers and drawn by a ram. Carols and tales accompany these rituals, recounting the road to Bethlehem and all that befell the shepherds who took it.

Philippe Monti's Christmas dinner pays homage to the old traditions in its use of fish and the best winter produce, olives, and the Ventoux's own winter wheat. His menu is elegant but rustic, as befits a mountain village celebration. Festive truffles appear in the first dish and quince dumplings star in the lavish display of the thirteen desserts.

•

CELERY ROOT AND TRUFFLE GRATIN WITH CURLY ENDIVE SALAD
Gratin de téléris aux truffes fraîches en vinaigrette

An unusual and colorful combination of gratin and salad, this dish makes original use of the Ventoux's fresh truffles. Canned ones can be substituted, providing truffle juice which can be mixed with the olive oil before sprinkling on the greens.

SERVES 6

2 medium-sized celery roots (celeriac),
   peeled and trimmed
1/2 stick (4 tablespoons) butter
Salt and freshly ground black pepper, to taste
1 fresh or canned, nicely round truffle (about
   2 ounces), with juice if canned
1 ounce Swiss or Gruyère cheese
Curly endive lettuce
1/2 cup olive oil

Cut the celery root into round slices about 1/3 inch thick. Using a sharp pastry cutter, make rounds 2 inches in diameter. For 6 servings, you should have a total of 30 slices.

Put the celery slices in a medium-sized saucepan and just cover with water. Add the butter and season with salt and pepper. Cook uncovered over high heat until almost all the water has evaporated and the celery slices are soft. Add more water if necessary during the cooking. Set the celery aside on a plate, handling it carefully so that the slices do not break.

Preheat the oven to 350°F. Brush the truffle well if it is fresh. Slice it thinly into 24 even rounds. In 6 horizontal stacks, alternate 5 slices of celery root and 4 slices of truffle, seasoning with salt and pepper as you go. Put a thin slice of Swiss on top of each stack. Stick

a toothpick through each to hold it together. Place in a small baking pan and bake until the cheese melts, about 10 minutes.

Arrange the endive in a ring around the outer edge of 6 plates. Sprinkle with olive oil and truffle juice, if available; season with salt. Place a truffle and celery gratin in the middle of each plate. Remove the toothpicks and slice each stack in half, from top to bottom. Let each half lie open to reveal the alternating black and white layers inside.

•

OLIVE-STUFFED FISH ROUNDS
Rouelles de mulet farcies aux olives de Nyons

The town of Nyons, just north of Crillon, is famous for its crinkly brown olives and its fragrant oil, the first in France to receive an official appellation of quality. Other ripe olives could be used, however, for this dish. For the fish, Monti uses red mullet (*rouget*), but fillets of red snapper or Hawaiian goatfish may be substituted.
SERVES 6

5 ounces brown or black olives, pitted
6 fish fillets (about 5 ounces each)
Salt and freshly ground black pepper, to taste
2 tablespoons olive oil

Reserve 12 whole olives for garnish and purée the rest in a blender or food processor.

Season the fish fillets with salt and pepper and spread the olive purée on them with a knife. Roll them up lengthwise and fasten with toothpicks to keep them rolled. With a sharp knife, cut each fillet crosswise into 3 or 4 slices. Reserve while preparing the vegetables.

Just before serving, heat the olive oil to medium high in a large skillet. Brown the fish rolls, turning once, 2 to 3 minutes on each side.

Winter Wheat and Sautéed Spinach
Risotto d'épeautre et poelée d'épinards

Chef Monti recounts that *épeautre*, which in English is sometimes called "einkorn," belongs to a family of "clothed wheats," a winter variety which does well in the climate of Provence. It has excellent nutritional value, but has been forgotten over the years because of its relatively low yield per acre. The farmers in the area of Sault, a town just east of Crillon-le-Brave, have rediscovered this grain and now cultivate it around the perimeter of Mont Ventoux. They have constructed a modern processing plant that produces both whole grains and flour. *Epeautre* can be purchased by mail from an importer of Provençal specialities in California (see page 153), but Monti says that pearl barley can be used for a similar effect.

Serves 6

4 ounces winter wheat or pearl barley
Salt, as needed
Olive oil, as needed (about 1 cup)
3 large onions, minced
1 small clove garlic, minced
2 tablespoons butter
1 anchovy fillet, in oil
1/2 cup water
1 1/4 pounds fresh spinach leaves
Freshly ground black pepper, to taste

Put the winter wheat in a large saucepan of cold, salted water. Bring to a boil over medium heat, stirring occasionally. Once the boiling point has been reached, simmer the wheat about 40 minutes. Remove the pan from the heat, cover, and let sit 10 minutes longer. Drain the wheat and reserve.

In a medium-sized skillet, heat 1 tablespoon olive oil over medium heat. Add 1/2 of the minced onion (1 1/2 onions) and the garlic and let cook until soft, without browning, 6 to 8 minutes. Add the winter wheat and stir to warm through. Just before serving, mix in the butter.

To prepare the sauce, heat 2 tablespoons olive oil in a small skillet over medium-high heat and soften in it the remaining minced onion (1 1/2 onions) without browning, 6 to 8 minutes. Add the anchovy fillet and 1/2 cup water. Stir and let reduce uncovered over low heat for 10 minutes. It should remain fairly liquid. Just before serving, pour the contents of the skillet into a blender or food processor, add 1/2 cup olive oil, and blend at high speed. Return to the pan just long enough to reheat.

Heat 2 tablespoons olive oil in a medium-sized, heavy-bottomed skillet. Add the washed and drained spinach leaves, stirring to coat with the oil, in several bunches as the volume reduces. Sauté quickly until just cooked, 3 to 4 minutes. Season with salt and pepper.

Make a bed of winter wheat on a large serving platter or each of 6 individual plates and arrange the fish slices on top. Dribble a little sauce over the fish and serve the rest separately. The spinach can be arranged around the outside of the platter or served separately.

•

The Thirteen Desserts of Christmas—Quince Dumplings
Les "Treize Desserts" avec les coings entiers cuits au four

The best-known feature of the Provençal Christmas supper remains its thirteen desserts, representing Christ and the twelve apostles, or the twelve lunar months of the year and the sun. The list of components varies somewhat from household to household. Poet Frédéric Mistral remembers dried apricots, raisins, almonds, figs, walnuts, plums, pears, apples, candied citron, quince jelly,

lumpy pears, they can be kept in storage like apples for winter desserts. Humble and unassuming, the quince undergoes magic transformation when cooked a long time with sugar, turning to a deep burnt orange or amber color which makes most decorative, as well as delicious, preserves. Beautiful jelly and paste are commonly made from quince juice and pulp respectively. But there is also a Provençal custom of baking whole quinces in bread dough, which has inspired Monti here for his more refined Christmas dessert. During the festivities at Crillon, as on family tables all over the region, the baked dessert is presented amid a lovely array of the other twelve.

6 quinces (5 to 7 ounces each)
6 tablespoons butter or as needed
1 pound puff pastry (store-bought or page 153)
6 tablespoons sugar or as needed
Vanilla ice cream (store-bought or page 155)
Dried fruit, nuts, oranges, and nougats,
  for accompaniment

the braided yeast pastry called *fougasse* (see a puff pastry version on page 153) or an oil-based cake, and two kinds of nougat, dark and light. Surely one of the finest delights of the Provençal countryside, nougat is made with lavender honey and almonds, and sometimes pistachios. The dried fruit is sometimes referred to as *les mendiants* (the beggars) in memory of the four mendicant orders of friars: walnuts or hazelnuts (filberts) allude to the light brown cloaks of Augustinian monks, dried figs to the dark brown of the Franciscans, almonds to the pale robes of the Carmelites, and raisins to the Dominicans.

Quinces are a commonly used winter fruit in Provence. Quince trees grow in many rustic hedges, turning from green to yellow as of October. The wild ones ripen later but are also more flavorful. Ressembling large,

Preheat the oven to 250°F. Wash the quinces well to remove the nubby fluff and make their skins smooth. Using an apple corer, remove the stems and as much of the core as can be reached easily without damaging the fruit. Place in a buttered baking dish just large enough to hold them and bake them until soft through but still firm, about 40 minutes. Test with a knife inserted into the center. Let cool completely.

Preheat the oven to 450°F. Roll out the pastry into 6 rectangles and wrap each fruit in pastry. Pinch to seal the seam. Sprinkle generously with sugar. Place on a buttered baking sheet and bake until golden, about 30 minutes. Serve lukewarm with vanilla ice cream, surrounded by an appealing assortment of dried fruit and nuts, oranges, and nougat.

The Sensual Garden

MENU

Asparagus, Clam, Tomato, and Salmon Salad
with Basil Vinaigrette
*La Salade d'asperges vertes et tomate fraîche et
palourdes, vinaigrette emulsionnée au basilic,
escalope au saumon fumé*

Nut-Crusted Chicken Breasts with
Sautéed Leeks and Wild Mushrooms
*Blanc de poulet pané de noisettes, poëlade
de poireaux, trompettes de la mort, émulsion
de leur jus relevée d'huile de noix*

Grape and Caramel Crisp
*Le Craquant de raisins au caramel,
croustillant de feuilletage*

Jacques and Laurent Pourcel   *Le Jardin des Sens*   Montpellier

65

Located midway between Spain and Italy, Montpellier is one of the most exciting and fastest-growing cities in all of France, blending an eighteenth-century past with an avant-garde present. Montpellier's face has been transformed by internationally known architects such as Ricardo Bofill, who designed the modern *quartier* called Antigone. Inevitably, the gastronomic landscape is changing as well. Many good new restaurants have sprung up, none so highly valued as the Pourcel brothers' establishment, Le Jardin des Sens.

Montpellier, the home of Europe's oldest medical schools and botanical gardens, is now a bustling center for tropical and Mediterranean agronomy, for communications research, and for cultural and leisure activities. Few metropolises of some 350,000 inhabitants can lay claim to two illustrious opera houses, an expanding university, and numerous summer festivals. The French themselves consider Montpellier one of the three best cities in the country for quality living. Of course the Midi climate and close access to the sea in a still unspoiled landscape add greatly to the city's appeal—the famous fishing port

of Sète and the resort areas of La Grande Motte are close by. And the old town still thrives, with its street markets (much admired by Elizabeth David), its lively cafés and theater, distinguished eighteenth-century townhouses, and the elegant Promenade du Peyrou.

Montpellier's energetic municipality has worked hard to reconcile its rich heritage with modern ambitions because the city has long had an in-between sort of image. Strictly speaking, it is not in Provence at all but in the Languedoc province (as are Nîmes, the Pont du Gard, and the entire southern right bank of the Rhône). The center of the Languedoc lies further west, however, around Toulouse, whereas Montpellier, like Nîmes, is often grouped with Provence with which it has common roots. Again, its geography is ambiguous, looking equally toward Italy and Spain.

Gastronomically, Montpellier cannot lay claim to the foie gras and cassoulet famous further west, still less to Bordelais refinement, nor to the colorful *aiolis* of Arles east of the Rhône. Yet it is very much a Midi city, considered by some as the most genuinely Mediterranean

French one (Marseille being judged too cosmopolitan).

Today, this in-between character and location have become an enormous asset. Montpellier is on the way to everywhere. Now connoisseurs come in increasing numbers from both the Riviera and Spain—about equidistant—just to have lunch at the restaurant of Jacques and Laurent Pourcel.

The Pourcels' establishment perfectly suits the new Montpellier. The Mediterranean remains the brothers' main inspiration, but the city's rich past inspires them, being a melting pot of cultures and influences. Montpellier was always open to other cultures: In medieval times, Arabic and Hebrew were taught at the university here. Yet the Pourcels are resolutely modern and have been touted as the chefs who will set the tone for avant-garde cuisine all over Europe in the year 2000.

Born in the countryside nearby of vintner parents, the twin brothers first set off on different paths, although both had determined to become cooks. Both had the best possible teachers: Michel Bras and Alain Chapel for Laurent; Marc Meneau and Pierre Gagnaire for Jacques. When the brothers decided to open a restaurant together, they wanted to return to home territory and sensibly chose a quiet, elegant, suburban neighborhood of Montpellier. They got their first Michelin star in a year, a second one two years later. Now Laurent does the meat dishes, Jacques specializes in fish and pastry. And they have been commended for the best desserts in France. Indeed, honors and awards have been showering down on them from all quarters.

The Pourcels' first building, with service for forty, proved too small. The brothers now have a modern restaurant designed to their exact specifications, twice as big, to fit the lot next door. Its huge walls of tinted glass can be opened or closed, shaded or not, quietly and efficiently according to changing weather and seasons. Tables sit on a series of gentle descending levels, like seats in an amphitheater to allow everyone an unspoiled view. The

décor, like the architecture, is ultramodern, all in soft grays, pinks, and white, with imaginative, futuristic bouquets—youthful and witty like the Pourcels and like the city itself. No pseudorustic wildflowers and copper pans here: Everything is smooth, clean, functional, well proportioned, comfortable. Never cold, but cerebral and sensual all at once.

The food, too, fits this description. The Pourcels seem to live for their art, their dedication is almost priestly. They are masters of technique, inexhaustible in their experimentation. Like the other contemporary chefs, they prize natural ingredients above all, but excel at original combinations of country vegetables (pumpkin, turnips, chard, spinach, mushrooms) with aromatic herbs—usually several vegetables for each dish. There are no sauces, only bouillons and natural juices. Fish is frequently roasted. Walnut oil often appears, as well as spices such as cardamom or paprika (sometimes served on the edge of the plate for those who wish to add more).

A lamb fillet comes with its sweetbreads, stewed artichokes, and broad beans, the small, yellow-fleshed potatoes called *ratte*—and mace-flavored juices. Sautéed lobster appears with tiny artichokes and asparagus tips and a vinaigrette with soy sauce and olive oil. Veal kidneys combine with a risotto containing dried fruit, leaf spinach, and curry-flavored juices. Rolled sole fillets are cooked with wild mushrooms, tiny onions and potatoes, and meat juices. The Pourcel's cooking is yet another version of the sophisticated simplicity that characterizes the new southern cuisine.

The desserts, however, are sumptuous and complex: A souffléd vanilla gratin contains chocolate chips and is served with a lemon verbena cream; an allspice-seasoned pear is matched with caramel ice cream; a chocolate and orange delight is enveloped in a "cigarette" spiral of pastry and served with a caramel with a hint of orange flower water.

The Pourcels' suppliers are often far-flung—a fact that also reflects Montpellier's in-between gastronomic status. Local producers are not yet used to catering to the special needs and small orders of a restaurant of this kind. So, although many of Le Jardin's vegetables come from the Montpellier farmers' wholesale market, some, like the zucchini blossoms, come from Nice. The olive oil is sent from Maussane, east of the Rhône. Their cheeses are brought by courier from a particularly good supplier in Bézier, much further west. The Pourcels' fish is generally from nearby Sète, though they prefer the Marenne oysters of the Atlantic coast to those closer at hand. Their wine list makes great show of the up-and-coming Côteaux du Languedoc, however.

All of the following dishes have appeared often on the menu of Le Jardin des Sens. Although some have been slightly simplified for home cooks, they reveal a quite special inventiveness. Each dish can provide the memorable experience that no one fails to have when visiting Le Jardin des Sens.

ASPARAGUS, CLAM, TOMATO, AND SALMON SALAD WITH BASIL VINAIGRETTE
La Salade d'asperges vertes et tomate fraîche et palourdes, vinaigrette emulsionnée au basilic, escalope au saumon fumé

Asparagus and smoked salmon are often associated in the cuisine of young chefs all over Provence, though here the clams play the star role. This unusual combination makes a refreshing summer entrée to eat in the garden.
SERVES 6

3 pounds medium-sized asparagus, peeled
Salt, as needed
1/2 cup white wine
3 shallots, coarsely chopped
2 pounds clams in shells
Juice of 1 1/2 lemons
Freshly ground black pepper, to taste
3 sprigs fresh basil, finely chopped
1/2 cup olive oil
1/2 cup peanut oil or safflower oil
1/4 cup boiling water
3 ripe medium-sized tomatoes, peeled, seeded, and diced
3 tablespoons chopped fresh chives
1/2 cup heavy cream
1 1/2-pound smoked salmon, cut into 6 slices, 4 inches wide
Toast, for garnish

Tie the asparagus into 4 even bundles and cook in a large saucepan of heavily salted, boiling water until just tender, 6 to 8 minutes. Using a slotted spoon, dip them into a large bowl of ice water, drain, and reserve.

In a large skillet, heat the white wine and the shallots over high heat. Add the clams and cook until they open, stirring as soon as the mixture boils. Discard any unopened clams, remove from their shells, and reserve.

In a small bowl, season the juice of I lemon with salt, pepper, and chopped basil. Whisk in little by little both of the oils and the boiling water to make a smooth vinaigrette. Set aside.

Cut the asparagus tips to a length of about 4 inches and the remaining soft stems into thin disks. In a medium-sized bowl, mix the stem rounds with the tomato dice, chives, cream, the juice of the remaining $1/2$ lemon, the shelled clams, salt, and pepper.

Divide the clam mixture among 6 serving plates, arranging each into a neat, 4-inch circle. Cover each round with a slice of salmon and arrange the asparagus tips decoratively on top. Sprinkle with the reserved lemon vinaigrette. Serve with toast.

Nut-Crusted Chicken Breasts with Sautéed Leeks and Wild Mushrooms

*Blanc de poulet pané de noisettes, poëlade
de poireaux, trompettes de la mort, émulsion
de leur jus relevée d'huile de noix*

The Pourcels are particularly imaginative with walnut oil and many varieties of wild mushrooms, both locally produced. This "sauce," a last-minute emulsion of cooking juices and oil, is also typical of their style. Fried potatoes make a fine accompaniment for this dish.
SERVES 6

1 stick (¹/4 pound) plus 2 tablespoons butter
1¹/4 pound fresh wild mushrooms
Salt and freshly ground black pepper, to taste
1³/4 pounds young leeks
1 egg
3 tablespoons water
³/4 cup all-purpose flour
*1 pound hazelnuts with their skins, roasted
  (page 155), skins removed, and finely ground*
*6 boned chicken breast halves (preferably free-range)
  with their skins*
*Chicken stock or broth (store-bought or page 155),
  as needed*
3 tablespoons walnut oil
Juice of ¹/2 lemon

Preheat the oven to 400°F. In a large skillet over medium-high heat, melt 2 tablespoons butter. When it foams, add the mushrooms, season with salt and pepper, and simmer until just barely tender, about 5 minutes.

With a slotted spoon, remove the mushrooms and reserve. Set aside the pan juices.

Bring a large saucepan of heavily salted water to a boil. Cut the leeks into ¹/2-inch lengths and simmer until tender, about 6 minutes. Remove from the pan with a slotted spoon and dip them immediately into ice water to preserve their green color.

In a small bowl, beat the egg with 3 tablespoons water. Set out 2 other small bowls with the flour and the hazelnuts. Season the chicken breasts with salt and pepper and dip the skinless side of each breast first in the flour, then in the egg mixture, then in the hazelnuts, pressing the nuts into place so that they will adhere during the cooking.

Melt 2 tablespoons of butter over medium-high heat in a large skillet that can go into the oven, or a flameproof casserole, and cook the chicken breasts skin side down until browned. Put the pan into the oven to bake until the nut crust is golden and the chicken cooked through, 10 to 15 minutes. Remove the chicken from the pan and set aside.

Scrape the bottom of the pan in which the chicken cooked and pour the scrapings along with any juice into a small saucepan. Add the reserved mushroom juices and, if necessary, add some chicken broth to make about 1¹/2 cups liquid. Reduce by half over high heat until about ¹/2 cup remains. Beat in the walnut oil and 4 tablespoons butter and adjust seasonings. Add a squeeze of lemon and set aside.

In a small skillet, heat the remaining 2 tablespoons butter and toss the leeks and mushrooms in it just to coat and reheat them. Place the vegetables on top of the chicken breasts and pour the sauce around. Serve at the table from the pan.

GRAPE AND CARAMEL CRISP
Le Craquant de raisins au caramel,
croustillant de feuilletage

The slopes around Montpellier are checkered with vineyards, and more and more excellent wines are being produced under the Côteaux du Languedoc appellation. Table grapes would be used for this delightful recipe. The chefs recommend the green muscat variety, which has a strong, sweet flavor. But any well-flavored variety would do.

SERVES 6

12 ounces puff pastry (store-bought or page 153)
2 tablespoons powdered sugar
Butter, for baking sheet
1/3 cup whipping cream, beaten until soft peaks form
1/2 cup thick custard cream (page 154)
1/2 cup granulated white sugar
3 bunches grapes (about 15 to 20 grapes per
  person), preferably peeled
2 cups half-and-half
Mint leaves, for garnish
Vanilla ice cream (store-bought or page 155), optional

Preheat the oven to 450°F. Roll out the pastry very thinly into a 15x20-inch rectangle. Cut out 12 circles about 5 inches in diameter, sprinkle tops with powdered sugar, and lay them on 1 or 2 buttered baking sheets. Bake until crisp and golden, 8 to 10 minutes. Transfer onto racks to cool.

In a large bowl, gently fold the whipped cream into the custard cream. Cover and chill.

In a small, heavy-bottomed skillet, heat the granulated sugar and 2 teaspoons water over very low heat. When it has turned straw-colored, add the grapes and turn with a wooden spoon to coat them. Heat 30 seconds longer. With a slotted spoon, quickly move the grapes from the pan to a plate. Pour in the half-and-half. Stir well to mix and slowly bring to a boil. As soon as the mixture boils, remove from the heat and set aside.

To assemble the dessert, spoon a thin layer of custard cream onto each plate. Top with a layer of grapes and a pastry round. Repeat these three layers a second time. Spoon over the caramel sauce and decorate with mint leaves. Accompany, if desired, with a scoop of ice cream.

A Market Gardener's Menu

MENU

SAUTÉED FOIE GRAS WITH MIXED GREENS
AND LEEK SPROUTS
*Escalope de foie de canard poelé, salade
de mesclun, pousses de poireaux*

PROVENCAL BASIL SOUP WITH MONKFISH
AND WINTER WHEAT
*Pistou provençal de lotte au petit épeautre
du Ventoux*

BRANDIED CARAMEL APPLES
*Chaud froid de pommes caramelisées, au marc
de Châteauneuf-du-Pape*

ALAIN NICOLET *Restaurant Alain Nicolet* CHEVAL-BLANC (CAVAILLON)

73

The Cavaillon wholesalers' fruit and vegetable market is the largest designated national market in France. Elizabeth David described it in *An Omelet and a Glass of Wine* as she saw it in the 1960s: Everywhere were mountains of melons and asparagus, strawberries, red currants, cherries, apricots, peaches, pears and plums, green almonds, beans, lettuce, green onions, new potatoes, and the first, freshly harvested garlic of the year.

When the retail market set up after seven, Elizabeth David bought the makings of the day's picnic: lush, ripe tomatoes, a goat cheese wrapped in chestnut leaves, sausage from Arles, pâté, black olives, butter "cut from a towering monolith," apricots and cherries. Thus well supplied, she set off to the nearby Luberon hills. For in the 1960s, this sensitive British observer of French ways deplored the decline in the quality of modest French restaurants. Today she might well be heartened by their revival. Instead of planning a picnic, she might well head down the road to Châteaublanc for an excellent meal *chez Monsieur Nicolet.*

Cavaillon remains an unassuming town of some 21,000 souls, just southeast of Avignon, close to the point where two important rivers converge: the Calavon leading towards Apt north of the Luberon hills, and the great Durance sloping off towards Aix-en-Provence to the southeast. It is a most strategic location economically, already much appreciated by the Romans (Cavaillon has a sculpted Roman municipal arch). Rarely mentioned in guidebooks (perhaps because it is possible to traverse it on a series of dull, modern loops without ever suspecting the old town), Cavaillon has achieved its own, quiet fame as a market center for specialty fruits and vegetables. Roman coins minted in Cavaillon already bore a horn of plenty on one side.

The town's modern prosperity dates largely from the nineteenth-century, when surrounding lands of the

Comtat to the north and the Alpilles plains to the west were heavily irrigated with water from the Rhône and the Durance. It was then that the cypress hedging so characteristic of modern Provence began to be used for windbreaks. Long, rectangular fields thus protected from the bitter northwind, the mistral, and crisscrossed by irrigation ditches, created in only a few years one of Provence's best-loved landscapes, a checkerboard rich with patterns, colors, savors. Small, intensive family-run farms produce artichokes, asparagus, strawberries, and melons—all manner of tender vegetables and salad greens. Acre after acre displays espaliered orchards, their flattened, lacy trees not much taller than the vines that grow on higher, unirrigated land beyond. Agricultural production in these privileged sites of the lower Rhône valley is now much threatened by imports, from Spain in particular, since much of their market depends on the precocity of their production. But for the moment, they count among the richest and most beautiful farmlands in France.

The name of Cavaillon is particularly associated with a variety of deep orange–fleshed melon. In 1864, novelist Alexandre Dumas was asked to contribute his works to the municipal library of the town. He agreed in exchange for a regular supply of the already famous local melons.

The vivid patchwork of the valley lands sets off the stark and somber Luberon range rising to the east. Everything in the valley is soft, in contrast to the harsh mystery of the mountain, with its pinewoods and olive groves. Full of wild grottoes, the rugged, wooded hillsides of the Luberon provided refuge for religious heretics for centuries, later for resistance fighters during World War II. Oppède-le-Vieux, where Elizabeth David went for her picnic, is the hill town closest to Cavaillon, first in a chaplet along the ridge of the Luberon. In the sixteenth century, the baron of Oppède led a particularly bloodthirsty repression of local Protestants. Today, when these villages count among the most chic addresses

in France, there is still an austerity, a wild romantic quality to them and their landscapes.

Alain Nicolet's restaurant in Cheval-Blanc, just outside Cavaillon, combines the best of these two worlds—mountain and valley. The old, stone farmhouse of imposing dimensions snuggles against the flank of the Luberon on some two acres of pinewoods and olive groves. But the network of tiny backroads leading to the restaurant (all very carefully and obviously marked) threads among espaliered apple orchards and fields of feathery artichokes, along streams and past the wonderful, ocher-washed, honey-colored *cabanons* that Provençal farmers use for storing tools in their fields. The riches of the region's best market gardens lie spread out at Nicolet's feet, protected by the abrupt rise of the ridge behind.

Alain Nicolet grew up just a bit further north, in Monteux, where his father was one of the most important suppliers of fresh fruit and vegetables in the area. His father dreamed of becoming a professional cook and encouraged his son's vocation at an early age. After training with the great Pierre Hiély in Avignon, then at

Condrieu, in Paris with Alain Senderens, and at several other prestigious establishments, Nicolet started his own restaurant in Cavaillon in 1983. He got his first Michelin star only two years later. Since then his dream has been to own a country inn. After many years of long preparation and planning, the new place opened in 1991.

Alain Nicolet is the professional's professional. Covered with honors and awards (including the title of Maître Cuisinier de France), he takes an active part in promoting Provençal gastronomy and encouraging the young. He works closely with the hotel school in Avignon and can be found at every public manifestation in favor of local gastronomy. In 1988, he encouraged local schoolchildren's interest in learning about food and prepared a gastronomic meal for them, about which they wrote reports. His regular menus include a modest one for children from which they can choose for themselves; and he has found that, in some neighboring families, when children are asked what they want for their birthday, they ask for dinner at Monsieur

Nicolet's. Now his own son, eighteen years old, is training as a chef in Avignon.

Nicolet's menus, which change weekly, present the whole gamut of the year's vegetable production, from the artichoke turnovers of the spring, to the partridge and cabbage salad in the fall. The cooking is perhaps more classic than those of many contemporaries. Many dishes are clearly inspired by old family traditions, if their contemporary renderings are original and lighter: hare nuggets in pepper sauce with wood mushrooms, for example, lamb with rosemary sauce, or pheasant salad with endives and a juniper vinaigrette. Here, too, a great variety of breads is made on the premises, like the walnut rolls which accompany the mixed salad, served with hot, breaded goat cheese.

The following menu offers good examples of classic Provençal preparations revisited, but always with a personal touch and an extreme care for the quality of preparation.

SAUTÉED FOIE GRAS WITH MIXED GREENS AND LEEK SPROUTS
Escalope de foie de canard poelé, salade de mesclun, pousses de poireaux

This very simple salad sets off fresh foie gras (see page 152 for sources in America). But it could be used as a basis for many other things: sautéed chicken livers or even poached eggs. Mesclun is a traditional Provençal salad mix (the word *mesclun* is Provençal, not French). Its mixed greens may include any number of seasonal variants—endive, curly endive, red or green chicory, mâche, or arugula. Or different sorts of lettuce. Some of its ingredients should have a "bite" to them, however; mesclun is never bland. Leek shoots or baby leeks, the very young ones available in spring or midsummer, can be found in many Asian markets.

SERVES 4

12 leek shoots or baby leeks
Salt and freshly ground black pepper, to taste
1/3 cup good quality wine vinegar
2/3 cup olive oil
1 bunch chives, finely chopped
4 cups mixed salad greens (see above)
14 ounces fresh duck foie gras
1 tablespoon butter

Clean the leeks carefully and steam them on a rack over simmering water in a medium-sized saucepan until soft, 5 to 10 minutes. Rinse in cold water and set aside.

In a small bowl, stir the salt and pepper into the wine vinegar. Beat in the olive oil with a fork and add the chives to make a vinaigrette.

Arrange the greens on one side of each of 4 serving plates, the leeks on the other side. Dribble over the dressing.

Slice the foie gras into 4 pieces. Heat the butter in a skillet just large enough to hold the livers and sauté them 2 minutes over high heat. Season with salt and pepper. Place a slice of liver in the center of each plate and serve immediately, with any extra dressing on the side.

•

PROVENÇAL BASIL SOUP WITH MONKFISH AND WINTER WHEAT
Pistou provençal de lotte au petit épeautre du Ventoux

Pistou is an old-fashioned sauce made with basil, olive oil, and garlic, the Niçois equivalent of the pesto of nearby Genoa. Nice did not become part of France until the 1860s. Just as its language resembles, but is not derived from, the neighboring Italian dialects, so its cooking shares a common heritage. *Pistou* is commonly thought to mean "basil" in the local dialect, but Jacques Médecin, the notorious mayor of Nice and a famous gastronome, insists in his cookbook that it means "pounded," as with a mortar and pestle. The Niçois word for "basil" is, he says, *balico*. In Provence, *pistou* is most commonly added to a thick vegetable soup made at the end of summer, when the garden offers its richest choice. Today's chefs in Provence make as many variants on pistou as they do on artichokes *barigoule*. Nicolet's version is a whole meal in itself, with the addition of fish and *épeautre*, the winter wheat of Provence. See page 62 for more information and page 153 for sources on purchasing the wheat by direct mail. Barley may be substituted.

SERVES 4

ALAIN NICOLET

4 tablespoons plus *1/2 cup olive oil*
2 medium-sized carrots, finely diced
2 medium-sized potatoes, peeled and finely diced
1 medium-sized zucchini, seeded and finely diced
3 ounces green beans, finely diced
2 medium-sized ripe tomatoes, peeled, seeded, and diced
3 ounces fresh white beans, shelled, or canned
  cannellini beans
Salt and freshly ground black pepper, to taste
Leaves of 1 bunch basil, finely chopped
3 ounces winter wheat or barley
14 ounces monkfish, anglerfish, or other firm,
  white fish fillets

Heat 2 tablespoons olive oil in a large, heavy-bottomed saucepan over medium-high heat. Add the diced carrots, potatoes, zucchini, green beans, and tomatoes, turning to coat with the oil, and cook 5 minutes. Cover with water, add the white beans (if using fresh), and simmer until cooked through, 20 to 30 minutes. (If canned beans are used, add only at the end of the cooking.) Season with salt and pepper.

Strain the mixture into a bowl, reserving both the broth and the vegetables. Put the broth with the basil, 1/2 cup olive oil, salt, and pepper in a blender or food processor and process until smooth. Return the broth and vegetables to the saucepan and keep warm.

Bring to boil a large saucepan of water. Add the winter wheat and cook uncovered over medium heat for about 35 minutes. Drain well and add to the hot basil soup 5 minutes before serving.

Cut the fish fillets into thin slices. Heat 2 tablespoons olive oil in a large skillet over high heat. Add the fish slices and sauté them until just cooked through, 2 to 4 minutes.

Spoon the hot basil soup, mixed with the winter wheat, into 4 soup plates and place the fish slices in the middle. Serve immediately.

BRANDIED CARAMEL APPLES
Chaud froid de pommes caramelisées, au marc
de Châteauneuf-du-Pape

Espaliered apple orchards stretch out in elegant rows practically at Alain Nicolet's doorstep. In this dessert, he would certainly use a marc (brandy distilled from grape pommace) made by his cousins at the Domaine de Chante-perdrix in Châteauneuf-du-Pape. In Italy and California, marc is also known as "grappa," but another brandy could of course be substituted.
SERVES 4

4 egg whites
1 1/4 cups sugar
1/2 cup all-purpose flour, plus more for
  rolling out cookies
1 stick (1/4 pound) butter, melted
2 tablespoons butter, for sautéing, plus more
  for cookie sheet
4 Golden Delicious apples, peeled, cored,
  and thickly sliced
1/2 cup marc (grappa) or other brandy
2 cups heavy cream
1 pint vanilla ice cream (store-bought or page 155)

In a large bowl, mix the egg whites with 1/2 cup of the sugar, then beat them into stiff peaks with a whisk or an electric mixer. Gently fold in the flour, then the melted butter, blending well to make a smooth cookie dough. Cool, cover, and chill.

Heat the 2 tablespoons butter in a skillet over medium heat and sauté the apple slices until golden. Sprinkle 1/4 cup sugar over the apple slices and cook until they caramelize, keeping careful watch that they do not burn. Pour brandy over the apples, stirring well, and set aside. The apples will be served lukewarm.

In a small, thick-bottomed saucepan, heat the

remaining $^1/2$ cup sugar over medium heat, stirring all the time, until it melts, boils, and caramelizes. As soon as it turns golden, add the cream, blend well, scraping the bottom, and let reduce over low heat until slightly thickened. Remove from heat and let cool.

Preheat the oven to 350°F. Roll out the cookie dough on a floured surface into a 10-inch square. Cut out 4 rounds, about 5 inches wide, and lay them on a greased cookie sheet. Bake them until golden, 10 to 15 minutes. Place an ordinary drinking glass upside down in a large bowl. This will allow you to shape the "baskets" while the cookies are still pliable. Remove the cookies from the oven and immediately mold each round over the bottom end of the glass, then set each, very gently, on a rack to cool. Each should now have the form of a tulip-shaped basket.

For the final assembly, spread some of the caramel cream on each plate. Place a cookie basket on each, containing a ball of vanilla ice cream and the lukewarm, caramelized apples.

Autumn Harvest

MENU

Fish Carpaccio with Vanilla Bean
and Olive Oil Dressing
*Saint-Pierre à la vanille et à l'huile d'olive,
façon carpaccio*

Scallop Sabayon with Wild Mushrooms
and New Potatoes
*Tian de Saint Jacques aux cèpes
et pommes Charlotte*

Truffled Sheep's Cheese
with Mixed Greens
Truffes de brousse en salade mesclun

Spiced Apple-Pear Compote
with Orange-Flower Pastries
*Pommes et poires à la canelle en compôte,
fougasse feuilletée à la fleur d'oranger*

REINE SAMMUT · *La Fenière* · LOURMARIN

This is a love story. Love of husband and family, love of creating and giving, above all, love of life. Food critic Christian Millau wrote of Reine and Guy Sammut: "These people are happy. You can see it, you can taste it." And from this atmosphere—the result of chance encounters and of modest endeavors—is now emerging one of the most promising young chefs of France: a woman, Reine Sammut.

Reine Sammut did not grow up as a country girl, nor as a nest maker. Her father was a custom's officer, and the family moved to the city of Avignon when she was a child. She had a solid, middle-class upbringing, went to a Jesuit school, and prepared to study medicine at the University of Marseille. Once her roommate at college invited her to spend a weekend in Lourmarin, where the friend's parents had a hotel and restaurant. The two nineteen-year-olds spent all their time peeling vegetables. It was fun, but not inspiring.

On another occasion, during her student days, she met a frizzy-haired guitar player by the name of Guy Sammut. He was vaguely studying Spanish in Aix and working in a crêperie over the summer. This was the early 1970s, when parents found it particularly hard to get their children to settle down and begin work on serious careers. Guy's parents feared he would abandon everything for music, so his father offered to set up his son in business—a small restaurant in Lourmarin, where the family owned property. On March 19, 1975, La Fenière opened for its first season.

The family's ace in the hole was Guy's mother, a woman of powerful character and an inspired—and determined—cook. She had catered for two years for the Franco-Scandinavian Institute in Aix, which at that time had no kitchen, so that Madame Sammut prepared all the food in her own home and took it to the institute by taxi. Her own mother, in Tunisia, had cooked for guests in her family pension.

Reine was still studying in Marseille, but wanted to help with the new venture. To practice, she worked part-time as a waitress in the cafeteria of the School of Pharmacy. Her old roommate taught her how to carry three plates at a time so that, over the summer vacation, she could serve in the new restaurant. But Sammut began to feel a bit guilty, watching Guy's mother get up at six every morning, sleep fifteen minutes after lunch while leaning on one elbow at table, then work until eleven in the evenings. Reine offered to help in the kitchen, where her first responsibility was making a range of simple desserts. The first season was a great success.

At medical school, in a class of hundreds, Reine Sammut placed 131st, but only 130 were chosen that year. This, she decided, was fate. Before the restaurant's second season, she and Guy were married, knowing that the villagers in Lourmarin would be worried by any unconventional goings-on. Her mother-in-law gradually began to teach her more and more cooking. Reine Sammut loved it, and soon found herself chief cook of the establishment.

La Fenière was still a rustic bistro with heavy earthenware plates and rough-hewn chestnut tables. In 1977, Reine's first daughter was born—on a Monday, the weekly closing day. She and Guy were still living next door, and everyone in the restaurant helped keep an eye on the baby while mama was in the kitchen.

Meanwhile, Guy had been developing his knowledge of wines. He became a representative for a vintner in Visan, a job that involved not only travel but also a good many gastronomic meals. In those days he would come home and tell Reine what he had eaten, and she would try to reproduce the dishes he liked best. Little by little, she added new items to her menu at La Fenière, under a new title: *Reine vous propose aussi* (chef's suggestions). But her major aim and inspiration, she insists, was her husband's pleasure.

In 1980, the Sammut's second daughter was born. A serious illness a year later meant that the child required

a special diet with no fat, no starch, and no sugar. Reine found time to make her special, delicious dishes every day, especially pastries, so that the child considered her condition a privilege rather than a privation. Two years later she was able to eat normally.

Today the Sammuts' eldest daughter is preparing for the Professional Hotel School, with a view to following in her mother's footsteps. By now, of course, she has seen its evolution from the family bistro to what the critics call a temple of haute cuisine. Already by 1985, Reine Sammut was recognized and acclaimed by the best guides, in spite of a location somewhat off the beaten track. Luckily Lourmarin has two luxury hotels and several charming pensions for visitors wishing to spend the night after dining.

Reine Sammut's original customers have followed her evolution, and she has sought out their advice and reactions along the way. Like many chefs, she is shy about going round the tables after the service. Instead, she sits and has coffee in the bar downstairs, so customers may stop to chat or not, on their way out, as they wish. She sparkles and bubbles and talks a blue streak—especially about her husband and family. It is hard to get her to tell about herself. Her gaiety is contagious. Shunning the traditional chef's toque, she sports a soft, white cloth cap that makes her look like a nineteen-year-old gamine.

As a self-taught chef sometimes gaining higher marks in the guides than much more celebrated colleagues, Reine Sammut is a living example of the link between old-fashioned, women's cooking of the bistro variety and contemporary gastronomy. So many of her male contemporaries lovingly recall a grandmother, or mother, who got them started. Almost all profess admiration for the role family cooks have played in maintaining country and regional traditions, while finding ingenious solutions to practical problems from day to day, out of necessity and economy.

Reine Sammut began her cooking career with her mother-in-law, then as a wife and mother herself. Then she single-handedly made the leap from this to the highly competitive world of haute cuisine—a move that for everyone else takes at least a generation. Today she regularly participates in all the professional meetings, competitions, manifestations, where the quality of her work is very highly regarded, winning many awards. Her husband is her greatest fan and promoter.

For his part, Guy has acquired an excellent reputation as a wine expert and is sommelier at La Fenière. There are some 350 wines mentioned on their list, all personally chosen. The Sammuts regularly organize tastings for specialists. Now they are planning to do olive oil tastings as well.

The Sammuts recognize the importance of choice ingredients. Reine now scours the local countryside, particularly rich in fruit and vegetables, for the very best products. It was her father-in-law who first took her to Martigues and introduced her to the local specialty *poutargue*, pressed gray mullet roe, among other coastal specialities. Her cuisine is now enriched by travel memories as well as local sources, and her husband's connections with Tunisia (where his family lived until 1948) have a role to play as well. Thus her celery spring rolls

with anchovy sauce use phyllo dough, but take their inspiration from the old Provençal *anchoïade*, where celery is served with anchovy sauce. But she is not a purist; her nuggets of venison with red cabbage, apples, and sour cherry sauce is an echo of her family's Alsatian origins.

Reine Sammut's small kitchen has become quite cosmopolitan; she takes on trainees from Japan, Greece, and Lebanon. She is drawn especially to the Mediterranean world, so rich in aromas, but feels the danger of mixing too many flavors in a single dish. And indeed, her hallmark is a rigorous simplicity. The desserts can be sumptuous—a bitter almond ice cream with hazelnuts or a rosemary sherbet. Reine Sammut discovered with much surprise, early on in her new career, that there was such a thing as a specialized pastry chef! Nonetheless, she continues to prepare all the desserts herself.

•

Fish Carpaccio with Vanilla Bean and Olive Oil Dressing
Saint-Pierre à la vanille et à l'huile d'olive, façon carpaccio

Carpaccio is typically made with thin slices of raw, cured beef. This unusual version uses fresh fish, takes just minutes to prepare, and has only three ingredients. The fillets must be extremely fresh, preferably from a fish caught the same day, and might be bought from a fishmonger specializing in fish for sushi.
Serves 6

1 vanilla bean
3/4 cup extra-virgin olive oil
1 1/2 pounds white fish fillets (John Dory,
  monkfish, or other very fresh, firm-fleshed fish)
Salt, to taste

Split the vanilla bean lengthwise and scrape the seeds into the olive oil with the point of a knife. Using a pastry brush, coat 6 serving plates with this mixture. Cut the fish fillets into extremely fine slices and arrange them on the plates. Brush each slice well with the vanilla oil. Salt lightly and brush again. Cover the plates with plastic wrap and refrigerate 10 minutes before serving.

•

SCALLOP SABAYON WITH WILD MUSHROOMS AND NEW POTATOES
Tian de Saint Jacques aux cèpes et pommes Charlotte

This simple but rich recipe is impressive in autumn, when scallops, mushrooms, and new potatoes are at their best. The Charlotte variety of potato chosen by the chef has firm, yellow flesh, and any similar type would do. The finished dish looks like a gratin, but today the young chefs rarely use long, slow baking methods. Dishes are usually browned at the last minute under the broiler or with a hand-held salamander, for a minimum of cooking and best preservation of flavor.

SERVES 6

1/2 pound new potatoes, peeled, cooked, and cooled
2 1/4 pounds fresh porcini or other wild mushrooms,
  wiped clean and cut into medium-sized pieces
3 sticks (3/4 pound) butter
Salt and freshly ground black pepper, to taste
24 large scallops
2 cups dry white wine
1 shallot, minced
2 egg yolks
1/2 cup whipping cream, beaten until soft peaks form

Cut the potatoes into pieces the same size as the mushroom pieces. Heat 2 tablespoons butter in a large, heavy-bottomed skillet over medium-high heat and cook the mushrooms and the potatoes together until golden, about 10 minutes. Season with salt and pepper and keep warm.

Heat 2 tablespoons butter in a medium skillet over medium-high heat and cook the scallops until golden, turning frequently, about 3 minutes. Season with salt and pepper and keep warm.

Preheat the broiler. Dice the remaining 2 1/2 sticks butter for the sauce. To make the sauce, put the wine and shallot in a small saucepan and boil over high heat until reduced by half. Remove from the heat and add the diced butter, 2 tablespoons at a time, beating with a wire whisk until slightly thickened. In the top of a double boiler, beat the 2 egg yolks, place over a pan of barely simmering water, and pour the wine butter little by little into the yolks, whisking constantly; never allow the mixture to boil. Remove the pan from the heat and fold in the whipped cream. Season with salt and pepper.

Divide the mushroom and potato mixture among 6 heatproof serving plates. Arrange 4 scallops on each plate and spoon the sabayon sauce over them. Put the plates under the broiler until the top just turns golden, about 2 minutes. Serve immediately.

TRUFFLED SHEEP'S CHEESE WITH MIXED GREENS
Truffes de brousse en salade mesclun

An amusing recipe, quite in keeping with the modern spirit insofar as it mixes simple country ingredients in an entirely new manner, with a view to texture as well as flavor.

SERVES 6

4 ounces canned truffles with juice
1/2 pound fresh ewe's cheese or feta, crumbled
* and moistened with heavy cream*
2 tablespoons balsamic vinegar
Salt and freshly ground black pepper, to taste
1/4 cup olive oil
3 to 4 cups mesclun or mixed, strong-flavored salad greens
* (curly endive, red chicory, mâche, arugula, etc.)*

Drain the truffles, reserving juice. Finely chop the truffles and spread them in a soup plate or shallow bowl. Divide the cheese into 6 equal parts and shape them into balls. Roll them in the chopped truffles, pressing lightly so that the truffles coat the cheese balls. For the dressing, mix about 2 tablespoons of the truffle juice with the vinegar, salt, and pepper in a small bowl. Then slowly beat in the olive oil with a fork or whisk.

In a large bowl, toss the greens with the dressing and divide among 6 serving plates. Place one cheese ball on each dish.

Spiced Apple-Pear Compote with Orange-Flower Pastries

Pommes et poires à la canelle en compôte, fougasse feuilletée à la fleur d'oranger

Autumn fruit is here accompanied with one of Provence's oldest pastries, the *fougasse*, its strips twisted into a leaf shape. Savory versions of the *fougasse* are sometimes filled with anchovies, olives, or bacon bits. The glaze of orange flower water is traditional for southern pastries, but another flavoring could be used. This recipe calls for strongly flavored apples and pears. If using blander varieties, a tablespoon of lemon juice might be added.

Serves 6

2 pounds cooking apples (Jonathan, Granny Smith, or Rome Beauty)
2 pounds Bartlett pears
3/4 cup sugar
1 cinnamon stick
12 ounces puff pastry (store-bought or page 153)
Butter, for greasing cookie sheet
1 egg yolk
2 teaspoons orange flower water

Preheat the oven to 425°F. Peel the apples and the pears and cut them into large dice. Put them in a large saucepan with all but 1 tablespoon of the sugar and stir to blend well. Add the cinnamon stick, bring to a boil, and simmer until the fruit is just barely soft and has reduced to the consistency of chunky apple sauce, about 20 minutes.

Meanwhile, divide the puff pastry into 6 diamond shapes. Make 5 slits lengthwise in each: 3 along the central axis and 1 on each side. In baking, these slits will open and the pastry will look like open fretwork (the traditional *fougasse* presentation). Lay the diamonds on a greased cookie sheet. In a small bowl, beat together the egg yolk, orange flower water, and the remaining tablespoon of sugar and brush the surface of the pastry diamonds with this mixture. Bake until golden and risen, 10 to 15 minutes.

Divide the fruit compote among 6 dishes, and place a golden pastry beside each.

Provençal Light

MENU

EGGPLANT AND BASIL MOUSSE
Terrine d'aubergine au basilic

ROLLED SOLE FILLETS WITH SORREL
AND TAPENADE
Enroulé de sole à l'oseille, une légère tapenade

CHICKEN BREASTS
WITH BRAISED SPRING ARTICHOKES
*Suprême de volaille en barigoule
d'artichauts printaniers*

SEASONAL FRUIT SALAD
WITH FRESH PROVENCE HERBS
Salade de fruits frais au parfums de Provence

PASCAL MOREL   *L'Abbaye de Sainte-Croix*   SALON-DE-PROVENCE

Between Aix-en-Provence and Avignon lies a stretch of country where rugged hills alternate with valley vineyards, small, elegant châteaux, and medieval monuments. Just north of Salon-de-Provence is an isolated abbey, sheltered by bare limestone cliffs and surrounded by intensely fragrant *garrigue* or scrubland. It looks out onto the whole of southern Provence down to, and including, the Mediterranean. This has become a Relais & Châteaux hotel, L'Abbaye de Sainte-Croix. Just minutes away from Aix, Salon, or Marseille, the hotel is a world of its own, a place of quiet retreat and repose on some fifty acres of parkland, of which four are regularly maintained. The rest has remained much as it was in the Middle Ages.

Of course in those days no Provençal population lived—and ate—more frugally than these remote monastic communities! This site's reputation dates back to the fifth century when a piece of the true cross was supposedly venerated on this spot. The first abbey was built here some four hundred years later, and still later belonged to the particularly austere Cistercian order, whose members often lived on acorns, nuts, and herb teas.

During the reign of Louis XIV, a nobleman became a hermit in a grotto on the same hillside. Here he practiced healing with herbs and plants. He had "only one servant" according to accounts of the period, wore rough-woven cloth, and subsisted on moldy bread. As the hermit's reputation spread, it drew great crowds. They received hospitality at the nearby abbey where, it is hoped, they had somewhat better fare.

Although religious communities returned to this monastery after the French Revolution, the abbey never recovered its former fame. Abandoned for decades, it was severely shaken by the earthquake of 1909. Then, in 1969, the Bossard family took over restoration of the abbey and eventually turned it into a hotel. Today it is laid out like a medieval labyrinth around a series of courtyards full of surprises. One ancient well has attracted mediums who claim it shelters a secret room full of books and manuscripts, though as yet no search has been carried out. Two fifth-century sarcophagi lie near it.

The Abbaye de Sainte-Croix today exemplifies the successful transformation of austere tradition into simple good living. Its twelfth-century chapel is being converted into a temperature-controlled wine cellar. Each hotel room has been reconstructed from two or three monks' cells, for space and modern comfort. All have terraces or a private garden. The furnishings are those of a well-off country home, unpretentious and solid, as if they had always been there. The vast dining room has kept its great stone vaults. Spacious salons cluster antique chairs around enormous fireplaces, blazing in the off-season when the hotel fills up with private seminars. In summer, of course, this mountaintop is delightfully cool; the hotel's formal and poolside gardens provide both sun and shade, privacy and festivity, as does the long, protected outdoor dining terrace.

In all seasons, this is a place to commune with nature, to escape into the wilderness—like the goat, gone wild, who can regularly be seen scaling the high rocks behind the hotel. One would never suspect the proximity of well-garnished stables, but horseback riding is one of the owner's passions and one of her hotel's best features. Even more discrete are the barnyard and vegetable gardens. The Abbaye de Sainte-Croix creates the feeling of a community living in peaceful independence, almost in another century—but this is of course an illusion. The modern world with all its resources remains at the doorstep.

The owner, Mademoiselle Catherine Bossard, had been working as a tour operator in Sri Lanka when she inherited the business from her father. Knowing herself inexperienced, she quickly formed a team of competent, well-trained people, over which she presides in the best tradition of a mother superior. Her chef, Pascal Morel, is responsible for the Abbaye's first Michelin star, and his wife is Mademoiselle Bossard's assistant—a new twist on the classic couple arrangement in restaurant management.

The Morels live on the Abbaye's premises, as does most of the regular staff. The wild and solitary setting seems to have created a strong team spirit, a sense of community also reminiscent of its old monastic days. There is a friendliness to the place that has nothing to do with public relations, echoing rather the ancient tradition of hospitality associated with monastic life. If northerners arrive on a day of sunny, early spring mistral, happy to be in the south, Mademoiselle Bossard will not refuse them lunch on the terrace, even if the tablecloth blows around a bit, or if she knows they will probably move indoors halfway through the meal.

Pascal Morel has been cooking at the Abbaye since 1986, after the usual tour of prestigious culinary establishments. Because his wife is Provençal, from Arles, they wanted to settle in the south. Sainte-Croix's blend of seclusion and solidarity suits his temperament exactly. When time allows, he gets his kitchen staff out digging in the vegetable garden, everyone lending a hand to produce the most tender vegetables—cherry tomatoes or local round squash called *coucourelles*. These make good soup, their shells providing tureens just the right size for two people. The garden also provides flowers for the dining room tables and fragrant aromatics like dill and coriander (the hillside suffices for thyme and rosemary).

For the rest of his needs, chef Morel has handpicked his suppliers, but he does not himself go off to market two or three times a week. He would rather, he says, be in the kitchen with his staff—some thirteen at any one time. Like many young chefs, Morel is shy about meeting the public, proud of his work but unhappy about seeming to solicit compliments at the end of the meal.

If life here has some monastic qualities, they are those of Rabelais' idealized Abbaye de Thélème, a haven for worldly as well as spiritual pleasures. And these center around food. Morel's style goes particularly well with fish from the nearby Mediterranean, tender vegetables, and fruit. And a light manner comes to him naturally. Sauces never smother, but gently accompany, like the vanilla and lime blend that sets off steamed red mullet fillets, served with carrots and onions. Fresh coriander blended with lime juice and olive oil is a favorite garnish. Monkfish is accompanied with blond lentils, and sea bass is simply dressed with basil and olive oil from the mill at Maussane. A delicious lobster salad comes with walnut oil and tarragon. Then there is the zucchini gâteau with smoked salmon and grated truffles. Typical of Pascal Morel, the following menu is rich in vegetables and also in techniques of presentation.

•

EGGPLANT AND BASIL MOUSSE
Terrine d'aubergine au basilic

Recipes for eggplant abound in southern French cuisine, differing from village to village. In his *Almanac*, Provençal poet Frédéric Mistral notes that ". . . in Sérignan, for example, they are stewed in oil, but in Carpentras, they are baked au gratin. In Le Thor, however, they are sautéed with garlic, onion and love apples [tomatoes], while in Maillane, they are prepared as fritters . . ." Pascal Morel's recipe takes inspiration from these old-fashioned dishes, but adapts them to contemporary

preferences for lighter food. The "love apples," however, remain, both in the baked terrine and the accompanying tomato coulis. Ideally, this should be baked in an earthenware or porcelain terrine, but a six-cup glass loaf pan could be used.

SERVES 4

2 pounds eggplant (about 4 medium)
Olive oil, as needed (about 1 cup)
Salt, as needed
1 pound ripe tomatoes, peeled, seeded, and diced
1/4 cup finely chopped fresh basil
1 shallot, minced
2 tablespoons finely chopped fresh chervil
2 tablespoons finely chopped fresh parsley
5 eggs, lightly beaten
1 small onion, chopped
1 sprig fresh thyme
1 bay leaf
1 sprig fresh parsley
Freshly ground black pepper, to taste

Preheat the oven to 425°F. Cut the eggplant in half lengthwise. Place the halves on a baking sheet, brush the tops with 2 tablespoons of the olive oil, and sprinkle with salt. Bake until softened, 20 to 30 minutes. Remove from oven and reduce the oven temperature to 325°F.

Let the eggplant cool slightly, then remove the flesh from the skin with a soup spoon and discard the skin. Chop finely and put in a large bowl with half the tomatoes and half the basil. Add the shallot, chervil, parsley, eggs, and 3/4 cup olive oil. Mix with a wooden spatula to blend well and adjust the seasoning if necessary. Spoon the mixture into an oiled, 6-cup terrine or loaf pan.

Place the terrine in a roasting pan and transfer to the oven. Pour enough hot water into the roasting pan to come halfway up the sides of the terrine. Bake until firm, about 1 1/2 hours. Remove from oven and cool to room temperature.

Heat 1 tablespoon olive oil in a small skillet over medium heat and cook the onion until soft, about 8 minutes. Add the reserved diced tomatoes, thyme, bay leaf, parsley, salt, and pepper. Bring to a boil, reduce heat to medium, and simmer until really thickened, about 1 hour. Remove thyme, bay leaf, and parsley sprig. Add the reserved basil and let cool. Transfer to a bowl, cover, and chill in the refrigerator.

Serve the terrine at room temperature. Cut slices directly from the dish, remove them gently to individual plates, and serve with the chilled tomato coulis, either arranged on each plate or separately.

•

ROLLED SOLE FILLETS WITH SORREL AND TAPENADE
Enroulé de sole à l'oseille, une légère tapenade

Sorrel is a leafy, sour-tasting vegetable common in Provençal cooking and available at better produce markets in America. In Provence, Mediterranean sole would be used, but in America, petrale or lemon sole could be substituted. Fillets of other firm, white fish of course could be chosen instead of the sole. Ask your fishmonger to throw in bones from the fish carcasses for the stock. SERVES 4

THE TAPENADE
3/4 cup pitted black olives
2 tablespoons anchovies in oil, drained
2 tablespoons capers, rinsed and drained
1/3 cup extra-virgin olive oil

THE SOLE
8 long sole fillets (about 4 ounces each) or
*   4 larger fillets, cut in half lengthwise*
1 bunch sorrel leaves, stems removed
Salt and freshly ground black pepper, to taste
6 cups fish broth or stock (page 155)
Juice of 1 lemon
1/2 stick (4 tablespoons) butter
Dill sprigs, for garnish

To Prepare the Tapenade

Purée the olives, anchovies, and capers in a blender or food processor. Gradually beat in the olive oil to make a smooth sauce. Transfer to a small bowl, taste for seasoning, cover, and set aside.

To Prepare and Serve the Sole

Spread out the sole fillets on a flat surface and lay the sorrel leaves over them. Roll up the fillets neatly and tie them with string. Sprinkle with salt and pepper and set aside.

In a medium skillet, bring the fish stock to a simmer. Poach the rolled fillets in it until just barely cooked, about 8 minutes. With a slotted spoon, transfer the fish to a shallow bowl, cover with plastic wrap, and keep warm.

In a small saucepan, heat $^1/_2$ cup of the stock with the lemon juice and butter over medium heat until the butter melts. Beat in 2 to 4 tablespoons of the tapenade to thicken very slightly and immediately remove the pan from the heat.

Divide the sauce among 4 serving plates. Cut each roulade in half so that the rolled pattern is visible. Place 2 fillets (4 halves) on each plate, presenting the rest of the tapenade separately. Decorate each plate with a dill sprig.

•

CHICKEN BREASTS WITH BRAISED SPRING ARTICHOKES
*Suprême de volaille en barigoule
d'artichauts printaniers*

Traditional, peasant-style *barigoule* in Provence was made with the earliest spring artichokes, simply stewed or braised. Thus the dish appears in René Jouveau's

La Cuisine provençale de tradition populaire and other old cookbooks. Later this specialty underwent exactly that progression Elizabeth David describes in Escoffier's adaptation of peasant dishes: a middle-class adaptation evolved made with older, larger vegetables, stuffed before stewing. Reboul's family cookbook *La Cuisinière provençale* from 1903, which includes French as well as Provençal recipes, contains both versions. Escoffier himself made *barigoule* with stuffed artichokes, and this is the version recorded by gastronomes outside Provence. Today's young chefs, however, go back to peasant sources. They also generally prefer shorter cooking times (large, stuffed artichokes take much longer than small, spring ones). Each chef now has his or her own version of stewed baby artichokes, just as each makes a variant on ratatouille and *pistou* (vegetable soup enriched with basil and garlic).

SERVES 4

THE BARIGOULE
4 tablespoons olive oil
2$^1/_4$ pounds baby artichokes, chokes removed
$^1/_4$ pound pearl onions, peeled
5 strips bacon, diced
Salt and freshly ground black pepper, to taste
$^1/_2$ cup water
1 cup white wine
1 tablespoon coriander seeds
1 bay leaf
1 sprig each fresh thyme and parsley
$^1/_2$ pound ripe tomatoes, peeled, seeded, and diced
Juice of 1 lemon

THE CHICKEN
1 tablespoon butter
4 large, boneless chicken breast halves, without skin
Juice of 1 lemon
Salt and freshly ground black pepper, to taste

To Prepare the Barigoule

In a large skillet, heat 2 tablespoons of the olive oil over medium heat and sauté the artichokes for 3 to 4 minutes. Add the onions and bacon, and cook over medium heat for 10 minutes, stirring occasionally. Season with salt and pepper. Add the water, white wine, coriander seeds, bay leaf, thyme, parsley, diced tomatoes, the juice of 1 lemon, and the remaining 2 tablespoons olive oil. Bring to a boil, reduce heat to a simmer, and cook until the mixture is thickened and the artichokes are tender, about 30 minutes. Remove thyme, bay leaf, and parsley.

To Prepare the Chicken and Assemble the Dish

Preheat the oven to 400°F. In an ovenproof skillet just large enough to hold the chicken breasts, melt the butter over medium-high heat. Brown the meat quickly on both sides, then transfer the skillet to the oven and bake until the juices run clear, 5 to 10 minutes longer. Remove the chicken from the pan and keep warm. Return the skillet to medium-high heat, add the juice of 1 lemon, and scrape up the brown bits from the bottom of the pan with a spoon. Season with salt and pepper and keep warm.

Arrange 2 or 3 tablespoons of *barigoule* on each of 4 serving plates. Cut each chicken breast into slices and lay them in a fan shape on top of the artichokes. Divide the lemony pan juices among the 4 portions.

•

SEASONAL FRUIT SALAD WITH FRESH PROVENCE HERBS
Salade de fruits frais au parfums de Provence

Aromatic herbs often appear in desserts in Provence today and lend themselves beautifully to ice creams and sorbets as variations on the traditional mint flavor. This recipe also takes its inspiration from the common use of herbs in infusions or teas to provide a new version of a classic dessert—a refreshing fruit salad.
SERVES 4

1 cup water
3/4 cup sugar
A sprig of any favorite fresh herb (rosemary, thyme, or lavender)
Assorted prepared, seasonal fruits (sliced apples, kiwi fruit, and/or strawberries; and/or whole raspberries; and/or orange and grapefruit sections)
Fresh mint leaves, for garnish

Combine the water and sugar in a small saucepan with the chosen herb and bring to a boil, stirring constantly. Immediately remove from the heat and let sit 10 minutes. Remove the herb and let the syrup cool.

In 4 soup plates, arrange the fresh fruit attractively and spoon the syrup over it. Decorate with fresh mint leaves. Serve chilled.

Lamb and Cézanne

MENU

PROVENÇAL VEGETABLE TERRINE WITH LAMB AND
LOVE-APPLE SAUCE
*Terrine de légumes de Provence confit au filet
d'agneau, coulis de pomme d'amour au basilic*

HONEY-GLAZED RACK OF LAMB
Carré d'agneau rôti lustré au miel de Beaurecueil

COUNTRY-STYLE ARTICHOKES
Poêlée d'artichauts de pays

ROSEMARY LACE WAFERS WITH HONEY
MOUSSE AND ANISE CUSTARD SAUCE
*Dentelles au romarin, crème d'anis, mousse
de miel de Beaurecueil*

RENÉ BERGÈS   *Relais Sainte-Victoire*   BEAURECUEIL (NEAR AIX-EN-PROVENCE)

René Bergès is a man of the earth. And it happens that he draws his sustenance from that same, blood-red soil that fed painter Paul Cézanne. Bergès' restaurant, the Relais Sainte-Victoire, sits just west of Aix-en-Provence, on the southern slopes of Cézanne's beloved mountain: the Montagne Sainte-Victoire, whose silvery-violet volumes and inexhaustible geometries provided the subject for dozens of canvases. Cézanne once exclaimed to a friend: "Look at that Mont Sainte-Victoire, what élan! What an imperious thirst for the sun! and what melancholy when, in the evening, that great weight falls to earth again. Those blocks were once fire, there is still fire in them."

And indeed, these famous slopes hide vestiges predating their emergence as mountains some thirty-five million years ago. The Montagne Sainte-Victoire is a protected site, not only because Cézanne painted it so often but also because its soil hides rich troves of ancient eggs belonging to dinosaurs and giant ostriches! Not to mention the digs of early Ligurian settlements, a population conquered by the Romans in the second century before Christ. This magic mountain is all earth and fire, from the layers of time it enfolds in its depths to the bonfires lit on its peaks every year to celebrate the summer solstice. Unfortunately fire struck the mountain once again in 1989, when many acres of its forestland were destroyed by an uncontrollable blaze. This sad event was commemorated by an exhibit of internationally known artists in Aix, in homage to Cézanne and to his beloved Montagne Sainte-Victoire.

Thus rich with legend and history, this stunning site with its deep red soil and high limestone sail draws many hikers, many pilgrims following in Cézanne's footsteps. Writer James Pope-Hennessey walked to the village of Beaurecueil in 1952 and described the mountain in its southern aspect: "It appeared to unfurl, or to unfold like a screen, revealing itself as a long range rather than a mountain, and seeming somehow biscuit-thin."

Perhaps Pope-Hennessey ate at a country café that the grandfather of Madame Bergès opened along that same road in the very year the English writer hiked there! The Relais Sainte-Victoire sits today on the exact site of the original café. This was later run as a restaurant by Madame Bergès' mother, Madame Jugy, who sometimes still participates at the Relais Sainte-Victoire, while running a smaller family pension, Les Cembres, at nearby Puyloubier.

Today's family unit thus consists of mother, daughter, and son-in-law. René Bergès has been happily adopted by this family of cooks, representing the third generation to cook on the same spot. Madame Bergès has chosen the traditional role of a chef's wife, receiving visitors at the relais and explaining her husband's menus. On a normal day, she works from nine in the morning to after midnight.

The cuisine here is also earthy, rich with the strongly flavored ingredients that mountain cooking provides: lamb and pork, aromatic herbs, truffles, full-bodied wines from the sunny slopes nearby (Côteaux d'Aix). Like the setting, the food is colorful, fragrant, and heady. René Bergès considers that cooking must be "gutsy" (*une cuisine des tripes*), at least in its initial

inspiration. One thinks again of Cézanne, who said as much about his painting . . .

At the same time, René Bergès adds a considerable measure of refinement to the traditional rustic fare of the hills. This is not, he explains, Provençal cuisine, but food with the perfumes of Provence. His personal inventiveness with the old ways has earned him the coveted title of Maître Cuisinier de France and high marks in all the French gastronomic guides. Eloquent examples are his two wonderful vegetable terrines: In one, a leek pâté coats a slice of foie gras; in another, a lentil mixture hides a choice fillet of wild hare. Both are served lukewarm with a subtle vinaigrette using oil in which wild mushrooms have macerated.

His menus are inventive, adaptable, and amusing. Most elaborate is the "Paul Cézanne Specialty Menu," where the chef helps customers choose a total of eleven different dishes, warning that at least three hours must be reserved for the experience. The meal might include a mixed fish plate with watercress cream and fresh pasta, spiced hare with cauliflower mousse, or a game turnover with port sauce and a salad of young, mixed greens. As a refresher at intervals between courses, Bergès serves a delicate rosemary sherbet.

At the other end of the scale, an economical lunch menu includes one dish, dessert, and wine. But there is also the menu, "Cuisine of Perfumes from the Heart," on which appears a "Cubist Medley of Provençal Vegetables" or sautéed fish with lavender butter. The "Menu of Provençal Savors" revives old-fashioned country specialties, like beef daube or tripe. There are also special menus for "Friends of the Table" or for "The Humbler Fish" (mackerel and sardines); another for customers in a hurry (the same for everyone at the table); and for children. Desserts are served from a sumptuously laden wagon. Clearly this is a chef who enjoys himself and wants his public to do the same.

And indeed, the relais' customers appreciate such blends of robust country fare and delicate invention. Many come from Aix, only fifteen minutes distant. One of France's most elegant urban centers since the sixteenth century, Aix is now famous for its prestigious opera festival in summer. Le Relais Sainte-Victoire is a great favorite of the Aix establishment for Sunday lunches throughout the year, but in July, you might well dine next to divas Jessye Norman, Barbara Hendricks, or Teresa Berganza.

René Bergès' choice of a lamb theme for the following menu is typical. Nothing could be more traditional than lamb in Provence and yet lend itself so well to new ideas. Sheep in Provence are no longer raised in small flocks. Today most producers of lamb have at least a thousand head. But they still practice the ancient custom of moving the sheep to mountain pastures for the summer so that they will retain the fine flavor of the wild aromatics they feed on. This practice has made Provençal lamb famous. Today Provençal producers around Sisteron have grouped together to acquire a protective label that would guarantee their lamb's quality, not only its origin but also the method of raising and age and manner of slaughtering. The best lamb must be killed at less than a year, preferably between three and six months, when still nursing but already feeding on herbs and fresh grass.

But of course lamb is a Mediterranean tradition, not only Provençal. René Bergès spent part of his childhood in Algeria and welcomes inspiration that he calls pan-Mediterranean.

•

PROVENÇAL VEGETABLE TERRINE WITH LAMB AND LOVE-APPLE SAUCE
Terrine de légumes de Provence confit au filet d'agneau, coulis de pomme d'amour au basilic

The idea of a lamb and vegetable terrine comes from Avignon, where the popes resided throughout most of the fourteenth century. A papal cook is said to have encased lamb in eggplant, in the shape of a tiara, and the resulting dish became known as *papeton*. But typically Bergès combines these familiar elements in an original manner. The terrine should be prepared two days in advance and chilled so that the flavors will meld. When you buy the lamb, be sure to ask the butcher for some bones for lamb stock.

SERVES 6

THE TERRINE

5 medium-sized tomatoes, peeled and seeded
Pinch of sugar
Salt and freshly ground black pepper, to taste
Olive oil (about 3/4 cup), as needed
1/2 onion, minced
1 red and 1 green bell pepper, roasted and
    seeded (page 155)
1 medium-sized zucchini, halved and seeded
1 medium-sized eggplant, peeled
1/2 pound boneless lamb loin (about 8 inches long)
Dried thyme, as needed
3/4 cup lamb stock (page 155)
1 tablespoon mixed chopped fresh herbs (basil, parsley,
    mint, tarragon)
1 sprig dried thyme
1 clove garlic, finely chopped
1 1/2 teaspoons (1/2 envelope) powdered gelatin
2 tablespoons cold water
3 thin slices cooked ham, each about 8x6 inches
    and 1/4 inch thick

THE COULIS

3 Roma (plum) tomatoes
1 tablespoon chopped fresh mint
1 tablespoon chopped fresh basil
1 tablespoon olive oil
Salt and freshly ground black pepper, to taste

GARNISH AND ACCOMPANIMENTS

Olive oil, as needed
6 small bouquets of fresh herbs (chives, basil,
    mint, tarragon)
Toasted country bread (optional)
Small bowl of tapenade (store-bought or page 93)

To Prepare the Terrine

Preheat the oven to 200°F. Put the 5 tomatoes with the sugar, salt, pepper, and 1/4 cup olive oil into an oven-proof dish just large enough to hold them, and bake for 2 hours. Reserve.

In a large, heavy-bottomed skillet, heat 1 tablespoon olive oil over medium-high heat, add the minced onion and let color lightly. Reduce heat to low and cook until soft, stirring occasionally, about 10 minutes. Remove and reserve onions.

Cut the peppers, zucchini, and eggplant into julienne strips about 3 inches long. In the same pan, heat more oil and cook the pepper strips in the same manner as the onions. Remove. Repeat with the zucchini strips and then with the eggplant, which should be tender but still crisp.

In the same pan, heat 1 tablespoon oil over medium-high heat and brown the lamb loin well on all sides, about 5 minutes. It should be crispy outside and pink inside. Season with salt, pepper, and dried thyme.

In a small saucepan, bring the lamb stock to a boil and add the chopped fresh herbs, a sprig of thyme, garlic, salt, and pepper. Simmer over low heat 10 minutes.

Dissolve the gelatin in 2 tablespoons cold water. Add to the hot stock. Mix well, cover, and chill until slightly thickened but still pourable.

Preheat the oven to 400°F. Lightly oil an 8 1/2 x 4 1/2-inch glass loaf pan or 1 1/2-quart terrine. Line the bottom, sides, and ends of the pan with the ham slices. Place a layer of baked tomatoes over the ham and gently flatten with a spatula or the back of a spoon. Spread the cooked onion over this and layer with pepper, zucchini, and eggplant strips. Place the lamb fillet in the middle, and cover with the remaining vegetable strips. Close the ham slices over the top. Pour in the lamb stock. The terrine must be well filled to the top; press on it to ensure there are no air holes. Set the terrine in a pan of hot water, cover with a sheet of aluminum foil, and bake until firm, about 25 minutes. Remove and let cool. Cover tightly and refrigerate for 2 days.

To Prepare the Coulis and Serve

Cut up the Roma tomatoes and push them through a sieve into a medium-sized bowl. Mix in the remaining coulis ingredients and adjust seasoning. Spoon a little coulis on each of 6 plates.

Cut the terrine in its dish into 6 slices (with an electric knife if possible), and place a slice on top of the coulis on each plate. Brush olive oil on the surface of each slice, and decorate with a small bouquet of herbs. Serve, if desired, with toast and tapenade.

•

HONEY-GLAZED RACK OF LAMB
Carré d'agneau rôti lustré au miel de Beaurecueil

This recipe and the following dessert make interesting use of the perfumed honeys produced in the hills of Provence since neolithic times. Ask your butcher for the first rack of eight chops in each case and have him prepare them for roasting, giving you the extra bones. Three racks is a generous serving for six and could be stretched to feed eight light eaters.
SERVES 6

3 racks of lamb (1 3/4 pounds each), trimmed, with
 extra bones
Salt and freshly ground black pepper, to taste
Olive oil, as needed
1/4 cup thick herbal honey (rosemary or
 thyme flavored)
2 cups white wine
5 cloves garlic, minced
Pinch of dried thyme

1 ripe, medium-sized tomato, peeled, seeded,
 and finely diced
1 stick (1/4 pound) butter, cut into bits
Country-Style Artichokes (following), for accompaniment
Fresh thyme and rosemary sprigs (optional),
 for garnish

Preheat the oven to 450°F. Season the racks with salt and pepper and rub them with olive oil. Place them in a roasting pan that can also go on top of the stove. Surround them with the extra bones and roast them for 15 minutes, turning them several times for even coloring. Remove from the oven (be careful, as they are now very hot). Using a basting brush, coat racks with honey on all sides, pressing it into the meat. Return the racks to the oven and let them turn golden, about 5 minutes. If during the final cooking, the honey in the pan starts to turn too dark, add a little water.

Once the honey has caramelized, take out the lamb and set aside, covered loosely with aluminum foil. Add the white wine to the cooking juices in the pan, scraping the bottom to loosen bits of caramelized meat. Add the garlic, thyme, and diced tomato. Put the pan on a burner over medium-high heat and reduce the sauce until slightly thickened, 15 to 20 minutes. Strain it into a saucepan and adjust the seasoning. Add the butter bit by bit to the hot sauce, beating with a whisk; do not let it boil. Keep warm.

Divide the racks into individual chops. Arrange 4 chops on each of 6 warmed dinner plates, surrounded by the artichoke mixture. Top with some of the sauce and serve the rest separately. Add fresh branches of thyme and rosemary for decoration if you wish.

COUNTRY-STYLE ARTICHOKES
Poêlée d'artichauts de pays

Prepare the artichokes before roasting the lamb and warm up to serve.

2 tablespoons olive oil
1/2 cup diced bacon or salt pork
6 fresh artichoke hearts, sliced and rubbed with
   lemon juice
1 cup sliced fresh wild mushrooms
Salt and freshly ground black pepper, to taste

In a medium-sized skillet, heat the olive oil over medium-high heat and brown the bacon until golden. Remove and reserve bacon. Add the artichoke slices and sauté them until tender, about 15 minutes. Add the mushrooms and sauté until they have released their juices. Return the bacon to the skillet, season with salt and pepper, and simmer another 20 minutes.

•

ROSEMARY LACE WAFERS WITH HONEY MOUSSE AND ANISE CUSTARD SAUCE
Dentelle au romarin, crème d'anis, mousse de miel de Beaurecueil

This light, subtle blend of rosemary, orange, anise, and honey flavors is very pan-Mediterranean. Each of the three components of this dessert—mousse, cookies, and custard—is delicious in itself and could be eaten alone or in other combinations, but their layered presentation is quite spectacular. The custard and mousse can be made a day ahead, but the lace cookies should be made the same day and the dessert assembled right before serving. Vanilla ice cream could also be served with this dessert.

SERVES 6

HONEY MOUSSE

1 1/4 cups milk
4 tablespoons fragrant herbal honey
2 egg yolks
1 tablespoon (1 envelope) powdered gelatin
2 tablespoons cold water
1 1/4 cups whipping cream

ROSEMARY LACE COOKIES

2 tablespoons butter, at room temperature, plus more
   for cookie sheet
2 tablespoons brown sugar
2 tablespoons granulated white sugar
2 tablespoons fresh orange juice
3 tablespoons all-purpose flour
1 pinch of dried rosemary, ground to a powder

ANISE CREAM

1 cup milk
2 egg yolks
1/2 cup granulated white sugar
1/2 teaspoon vanilla extract
Few drops anise extract

Fresh rosemary sprigs, for garnish

To Prepare the Mousse

Bring the milk and 3 tablespoons of the honey slowly to a boil in the top of a double boiler over simmering water. In a heatproof bowl, beat the egg yolks until lemon colored. When the milk and honey mixture is about to boil, pour it over the egg yolks, stirring all the time to mix well.

Return the custard mixture to the top of the double boiler and heat gently over simmering water without boiling. When the mixture thickens slightly and coats a spoon, remove from the heat. Dissolve the gelatin in 2 tablespoons cold water, and stir into the

RENE BERGÈS

custard. Transfer to a large mixing bowl and let set until cool, slightly gelatinous, but still fluid.

In another large bowl, whip the cream until soft peaks form. Fold the whipped cream into the custard and pour the mousse into an 8-inch, flat-sided dish or cake pan to make a layer about $1/2$ inch deep. Before serving, cut out 12 circles, each about 2 inches in diameter, with a cookie cutter.

To Prepare the Cookies

In a large mixing bowl, using a fork, cream together the butter with the two sugars until smooth. Add the orange juice little by little, stirring all the while. Blend in the flour and the rosemary, mixing well. Cover and refrigerate for 1 hour.

Preheat the oven to 400°F and butter 2 cookie sheets. With a teaspoon, drop 9 mounds of cookie dough on each sheet (spaced several inches apart) and flatten into circles with a wet finger. (The cookies will spread to about $1^1/2$ inches in diameter after baking.) Bake until nicely golden, 4 to 5 minutes. Be careful, as they brown very quickly. Remove from the oven and let sit 1 to 2 minutes, then transfer with a spatula to a cake rack to cool. You must work fast when the cookies are firm enough to keep their shape as you remove them, but not yet brittle.

To Prepare the Anise Cream

Scald the milk in the top of a double boiler, over simmering water. In a heatproof mixing bowl, beat the egg yolks with a whisk until lemon colored, then add the sugar and beat again. Pour the hot milk slowly over the egg yolks, stirring constantly, then return the custard mixture to the double boiler. Cook gently without boiling until the mixture thickens slightly and coats a spoon. Remove from the heat and add the vanilla and anise extracts and beat lightly. Strain and set aside to cool.

To Assemble the Dessert

At the time of serving, lay a cookie circle on each of 6 serving plates, top with a round of honey mousse, then another cookie, then another round of mousse. At this stage, put a small dab of honey in the center of the mousse circle and carefully place on top a third rosemary circle. Spoon 1 or 2 tablespoons of anise cream over the top of each dessert and serve the rest separately. Garnish desserts with rosemary sprigs.

Waterfront Cuisine from Old Marseille

MENU

Pumpkin Ravioli with Mussels Marinière
Ravioli de potiron et sa marinière de moules

Stewed Garlic Mackerel
with Spring Vegetables
Pot-au-feu de maquereau

Caramel Orange Cream
Crème à l'orange caramelisé

RAYMOND ROSSO   *Les Arcenaulx*   MARSEILLE

"Marseille the magnificent, the southern town par excellence," wrote Stendhal after his visit in 1837. He recalls that Tacitus described the city as "a happy mixture of Greek urbanity with Gallic temperance."

What the Roman historian wrote still holds true today: Marseille is very Provençal, but it is also very urbane, and it has a character all its own. The city remains a window on the world for old Provence, a place where the strongly rooted traditions of a region with great character meet up with foreign influences of every description. It is true that some of the city's activities make bad headlines; these unfortunately obscure its continuing role as a lively center for trade and exchange, not only of goods but of culture.

Today Marseille's heart beats nowhere stronger than in the cultural complex called Les Arcenaulx. And it is here, in the restaurant of the same name, that Raymond Rosso provides imaginative food for Marseille's leading figures as well as for cosmopolitans.

The city's history began with its port, a particularly deep inlet or *calanque* that, until the early part of this century when it was filled in, could be navigated right into the heart of town. Here legend has it that the Greek sea captain Protis was chosen by a Ligurian princess to be her husband, sometime before 600 B.C., thus founding the city's first international trade alliance. Greeks from Phocea opened up trading centers all along the coast; today French newspapers still refer to Marseille

as "the Phocean city." It was the Greek merchants of Massalia (as it was then known) who called in their new allies, the Romans, to protect their trade. These "allies" of course took over and stayed for centuries.

Sea commerce brought many ups and downs. Marseille had the bad luck to support Pompey in his war with Julius Caesar, and the winning general shifted his trade center to Arles. With the Crusades, however, the city regained its prominence. Then the bubonic plague arrived through the port of Marseille in the fourteenth century. The discovery of America led to a long decline in favor of Atlantic ports. But the conquest of Algiers, the suppression of Barbary pirates, and the opening of the Suez Canal made mid-nineteenth-century Marseille a booming colonialist port and created the base of its present economy. Three small museums in old houses around the old port—the Musée du Vieux Marseille, the Musée d'Histoire de Marseille, and the Musée des Docks Romains—make this rich past live again.

Trade and fishing were long protected here by a heavy military establishment, which made Marseille a prison city for centuries. Louis XIV condemned thousands of Protestants to man the famous galley ships as convicts. In the eighteenth century, the galleys were moved to Toulon. All the original constructions associated with their presence in Marseille have disappeared with the exception of one elegant building, known as the Governor's House. Some years ago, the city decided to restore this area situated south of the old port, along the Rive Neuve. The old fishmarket was turned into an active theater. But when it came to tearing down the military buildings that had housed the galleys' administrators, two sisters from an old Marseille bookselling family, Jeanne and Simone Laffitte, organized the neighborhood in protest.

Since the 1920s, this part of town had been a favorite refuge for bohemian artists and writers, including Marcel Pagnol (whose saga about the Marseille sailor Marius is a great classic of Provençal literature). Craftsmen of all kinds—sponge makers, fish dryers—existed side by side with the intellectuals. There was the painter Ambrogiani, who first became known in this part of town as the postman! An influential literary journal, *Les Cahiers du Sud,* was produced from an attic.

The Laffitte sisters were so successful that they have been able to create in the former governor's mansion one of the country's most celebrated cultural meccas, the complex today called Les Arcenaulx. It is built around a cobbled, central lane, half open to the sky though crisscrossed by picturesque, Piranese-like arches and passageways on the upper stories. On either side is a series of large, square rooms with rough stone walls and beamed or vaulted ceilings. Each has its own special usage: One giving onto the street is a shop for decorative objects having to do with food and wine (*les arts de la table*). On the other side is the restaurant and kitchens. Three rooms house the Laffitte bookstore (current, general, and antiquarian books). Three others are reception rooms and art galleries, each in a different style and dedicated to a different author: Rimbaud (who died in Marseille in 1891 of gangrene on his return from Abyssinia), Colette (who wrote so beautifully of Provence), and Proust (the buildings still belong to his descendants). All manner of poetry readings, small concerts, and other cultural events take place here. Simone Laffitte oversees this side of things including the restaurant, while Jeanne runs the highly successful publishing house, whose offices are upstairs.

Seldom has the "art of living" been so rich and varied. And at its heart lies the restaurant, where some two hundred people eat daily around intimate tables in two long, interconnecting rooms hung with red draperies. The atmosphere is convivial, even theatrical—a sea of Phocean faces drawn from Marseille's various elites: business, intellectual, journalistic. Everyone talks with animation, including the tough, chatty waiters.

The atmosphere is bistro—swift service for busy people, but jolly, lively, and unpretentious: a cozy, comfortable drawing room over which presides Simone Laffitte, a birdlike, attentive, and maternal presence with a word for everyone.

However engrossing the talk around these tables, no one neglects the food. Spiritual and earthy nourishment are inseparable throughout Les Arcenaulx, in the long-standing tradition of Marseille. (Stendhal much admired one local woman, known for her wit even in Paris, who held his interest for some time with a discussion of chickpeas!) At Les Arcenaulx, the food itself is witty: All the *coupes* on the ice cream menu have literary names. The traditional Mont Blanc becomes the Magic

Mountain, while the Madame Bovary is composed of green apple sherbet, Calvados, and—pepper.

An experienced and demanding public now confronts the new chef of Les Arcenaulx, Raymond Rosso. But he is a local boy, who loves the city for its theatrical conviviality. He trained at le Grand Véfour in Paris, at the Oustau de Baumanière in Les Baux, and at Passédat, a great fish restaurant up the coast, among others, and was formerly chef de cuisine at La Sapinière in Quebec. (There, true to his philosophy of exploring local resources, he experimented with beans and maple syrup.)

Rosso's new menu maintains the bistro tradition by keeping old Provençal favorites in their traditional guise: fish soup, little stuffed vegetables, tripe, all the local fish. But now there is also a fresh note, more pan-Mediterranean: The cod *brandade* is served with a leek velouté; sea bass is poached in red wine and garnished with an anise-flavored, sweet potato purée; grilled lamb comes with cumin and a chickpea flan. There is a special "market" menu with lobster in citrus sauce or carpaccio of beef with beet chips. The traditional Provençal menu now offers, as an alternative to dessert, a cumin-flavored, goat cheese soup. And each day, two new dishes are chosen by the sommelier to go with specially proposed wines.

The following menu reveals the same ingenuity with common ingredients, nothing fancy nor fussy. Strong flavors, witty associations, beautiful presentations—Rosso's cuisine confirms M.F.K. Fisher's contention that the cuisine of Marseille has unique character: "Freshly caught fish, scaly or in the shell, have a different flavor and texture and SMELL there than in any other port in the world…intense and assertive, no matter how delicate." But if these flavors are inimitable, Raymond Rosso's taste combinations could work anywhere, as long as fresh, good quality, local ingredients can be found. Marseille is not the only port in the world with good mackerel, mussels, or sardines! This is still an urbane cuisine, open onto the outside world.

PUMPKIN RAVIOLI WITH MUSSELS MARINIÈRE
Ravioli de potiron et sa marinière de moules

The old-fashioned dish of mussels in white wine is enriched here with pumpkin ravioli, for an original contrast of textures as well as flavors. Pumpkin is commonly found in Provençal cuisine, as a soup or a gratin, and is usually enlivened with garlic as here. The most commonly used Provençal variety of pumpkin is less dense than most American equivalents, however, and you may need to add a few tablespoons of water during cooking. Chef Rosso uses regular pasta in his version of the ravioli, but Chinese wonton wrappers instead of pasta make this dish much faster and simpler for family cooking.

SERVES 4

THE RAVIOLI
2 tablespoons olive oil
1 pound pumpkin or other winter squash, peeled,
    seeded, and cut into small pieces
1/2 clove garlic, minced
Salt and freshly ground black pepper, to taste
1 pinch ground nutmeg (preferably freshly grated)
32 wonton wrappers (each about 3 1/2 inches square)

THE MUSSELS
1/4 cup minced Italian parsley leaves
2 cloves garlic, minced
4 shallots, minced
2 tablespoons olive oil
1 pound mussels in shells, scrubbed and
    beards removed
1/2 cup white wine
1/2 cup heavy cream
1 ripe tomato, peeled, seeded, and diced
1 bunch chives, trimmed and cut into
    3/4-inch lengths

To Prepare the Ravioli

In a large, heavy-bottomed pan, heat 2 tablespoons olive oil and add the pumpkin with the 1/2 clove garlic, salt, pepper, and nutmeg. Stir from time to time until the mixture melts down into a purée, 30 to 45 minutes, depending on density. Set aside and adjust the seasoning; it should be well seasoned.

Lay a wonton wrapper on the work surface and put a spoonful of pumpkin in the center. Brush the edges with cold water and cover with another wonton wrapper. Press out the air if any, and press down on the edges. Using a 3-inch cookie cutter or ravioli cutter, make a neat circle and set aside. Repeat 15 times.

Heat a large pot of salted water until just boiling and add the ravioli (do not crowd). Cook (in batches if necessary) at a slow boil until they rise to the surface of the water, about 2 minutes. Drain thoroughly and keep warm.

To Prepare the Mussels and Serve

Mix together the chopped parsley, 2 cloves garlic, and shallot. Heat 2 tablespoons olive oil in a large skillet and cook the herb mixture over low heat for a few minutes, so that it softens without browning. Add the mussels and white wine and stir for 1 minute. Pour the cream into the pan, cover, and simmer 5 minutes. Remove the mussels and discard any that do not open. Remove the rest from their shells and reserve. Strain and reserve juices.

In each of 4 heated serving plates, set 4 raviolis. Put a small mound of mussels in the center, and pour over some of the strained cooking juices. Decorate with tomato dice and chives. Serve immediately.

STEWED GARLIC MACKEREL WITH SPRING VEGETABLES
Pot-au-feu de maquereau

Mackerel is a poor man's fish, like sardines, too strongly flavored for the traditional ways of preparing that great Marseille specialty—the fish soup or stew called bouillabaisse. But there are old Provençal versions of mackerel soup as well. Rosso calls this a *pot-au-feu* because the final result resembles the traditional mix of beef and vegetables served in their broth which usually goes by that name. But while the meat version is achieved by long, slow cooking, this recipe is very quick to make and assemble. If your fishmonger fillets the mackerel for you, be sure to ask for the backbones too.
SERVES 4

4 small turnips with their leaves
4 small carrots with their leaves
Salt as needed
4 celery hearts or 2 large bunches, all stems and outer
    leaves removed, hearts cut in two
4 mackerel (3/4 pound each), filleted with
    bones reserved
5 tablespoons extra-virgin olive oil
4 green onions, minced
1/2 cup dry white wine
4 cloves garlic, minced
2 sprigs fresh basil plus 16 pretty, fresh basil leaves
1 tablespoon sherry vinegar
Freshly ground black pepper, to taste
8 cherry tomatoes, for garnish

Peel turnips and carrots, leaving on about 1 inch of the leaves. Bring about 2 quarts of salted water to a strong boil and cook the carrots, then the turnips, then the celery, separately. As each is cooked, remove from the boiling water and plunge briefly into a bowl of ice water. Set aside and reserve also the cooking water.

Rinse the mackerel bones under cold water. Heat I tablespoon of the olive oil in a medium-sized, heavy-bottomed saucepan. Add minced green onions and fish bones and cook over low heat until the onions are soft, about 5 minutes. Add about 4 cups of the reserved vegetable cooking water and the wine. Bring to a boil and skim off any surface film. Reduce the heat and simmer about 20 minutes. Remove from heat, add the minced garlic and basil sprigs, and let sit for 1/2 hour to infuse. Strain broth into a medium-sized skillet and set aside.

In a large, heatproof bowl, mix the vinegar with salt and pepper. Add the remaining olive oil to make a vinaigrette and set aside. (The broth will later be added to the same bowl.)

Reheat the reserved fish and vegetable broth in skillet over medium-high heat and poach the mackerel fillets until just barely cooked, about 3 minutes. Remove the fish from the pan with a slotted spoon and keep warm. Add the vegetables to the hot broth, just to reheat them. Remove them and arrange with the fish in 4 heated serving dishes.

Quickly beat the hot broth into the reserved vinaigrette, and pour some into each serving dish. Decorate with basil leaves and cherry tomatoes and serve immediately.

CARAMEL ORANGE CREAM
Crème à l'orange caramelisé

Every chef today has his version of crème brûlée; orange zest and mint make for an interesting variant here. A good version can be made with fewer egg yolks, however, or a mixture of whole eggs and yolks, but it will be less extravagantly rich.
SERVES 4

10 egg yolks or 5 yolks and 3 whole eggs
6 tablespoons granulated white sugar
2 tablespoons flour
Grated zest of two oranges
2 cups milk
3/4 cup dark brown sugar
2 tablespoons chopped fresh mint

In a large bowl, using a whisk, beat first the whole eggs, if used, then beat in the egg yolks, then add the white sugar and beat steadily until the mixture turns pale yellow. Sprinkle the flour and grated orange zest over the contents of the bowl and stir in well.

Scald the milk in the top of a double boiler over simmering water, and gradually add it to the egg mixture, stirring to blend well. Pour everything back into the double boiler and cook over simmering water until the mixture thickens slightly, about 5 minutes. Do not allow it to boil.

Pour the custard into 4 heatproof 6-inch ramekin or gratin dishes 6 inches wide and let cool. (Cover and refrigerate until serving time if making ahead.)

Preheat the broiler. Sprinkle 3 tablespoons brown sugar over the top of each custard. Put the custard dishes in a shallow baking pan and surround with ice. Slip them under the hot broiler until the brown sugar caramelizes. Turn the dishes during this process for even browning. Let cool slightly, and garnish with mint before serving.

117

RAYMOND ROSSO

Southern Seafood

MENU

BARIGOULE OF GARDEN VEGETABLES
WITH CLAMS
Barigoule de "tous les légumes" aux coquillages

HERBED SARDINE FRITTERS
WITH RED PEPPER PURÉE
Beignets legers de sardines aux feuilles aromatiques,
purée de poivrons doux

STEWED FIGS WITH MUSCAT WINE
AND FENNEL
Grosses figues mauves au Beaumes-de-Venise,
infusion de fenouil

LAURENT TARRIDEC   *Hôtel Les Roches*   LE LAVANDOU

An old Provençal proverb would have it that fish always swim twice: first in water, then in oil. The first refers of course to their natural habitat, the second to their culinary preparation in that green-golden nectar produced by the olive orchards rising high above the Mediterranean. Sea and mountain are the two poles of life in Provence—and not only for fish!

On the coast of the Var department, between Hyères and Saint-Tropez, the descent from mountain to sea is especially steep. Inland rises the Massif des Maures, named not, as is commonly thought, for the Moors or Saracens (who occupied much of this area between the eighth and the tenth centuries), but for *mauro*, a Provençal word meaning "dark" or "deep." This epithet arose either because the rocks of these mountains (a mixture of quartz, schist, and granite) absorb rather than reflect light, or because of its densely forested slopes of pine, chestnuts, and cork oak. In any case, their rolling heights provide shelter from strong winds and create a landscape full of flowers. The coastal communities of Le Lavandou and Bormes-les-Mimosas together form a single resort area, nearly overwhelmed in February by the pungent odor of fuzzy, yellow mimosa, descendants of trees that Napoleon III's soldiers brought back as booty from Mexico. But there are also cistus, eucalyptus, wild broom, arbutus, and of course the silvery crowns of olive trees.

At the foot of these hills, Les Roches hotel and restaurant stands with its feet in the water. A striking, modern building on several levels, it stretches between the coast road above and the broad jetty below, so that customers may arrive as easily by boat as by car. The hotel's angular white walls are set off by exotic pocket gardens, cacti, and bougainvillea—brilliant colors set against grays and greens around the central stairwell, the dining terrace, and the discrete, shaded patios adjoining the rooms, each of which is like a small apartment. The long dining room has a panoramic view of the sea.

Through the centuries, the sea has brought wave after wave of exotic folk to the Var coast—starting with the first known inhabitants, the Ligurians of the Bormani tribe. They were followed by Phoenicians, Etruscans, Greeks, who set up a chaplet of trading posts along the

LAURENT TARRIDEC

coast, and finally the Romans, whose presence profoundly transformed the culture and language. Still later, barbarian tribes came from the north, and Moorish pirates from the south. The nearby fortress of Brégançon, now a residence for the French president, was first built as a bastion against Saracen invaders. High fortified hill towns with stunning views once offered refuge to local populations plagued with pirates for centuries on end. No wonder one historian has described the inhabitants of this land as clinging tenaciously to their rocks like shellfish.

Local inhabitants have earned their livelihood for centuries with their nets. But fishermen of the Var, unlike those of the Atlantic ports, never became famous as explorers. The sea has generally meant danger more than adventure. Another Provençal proverb says *Lauso la mare et tent'n terro* (Praise the sea and stay on land).

Today, sea and land coexist more or less peacefully, now that "invaders" have other, faster means of transport! The local tourist office promotes all manner of sports activities in the region on both sea and land. Throughout the year, a series of sailing competitions brings enthusiastic crowds, including the "Frozen Feet Regatta" in February. Bormes-les-Mimosas still has a double identity as a twelfth-century mountain village and as a seaport. Bormes and Le Lavandou share some twenty kilometers of coastline composed of sandy beaches alternating with rugged inlets or *calanques*, jagged points of purple-red porphyry rock rising from the turquoise waves. A newly opened public garden and plant conservatory, the Domaine du Rayol, lies just a few kilometers down the coast from the Hôtel Les Roches on just such an inlet.

Today's communities preserve their colorful folklore in festivities like the carnival of early spring with its flower-decked parades. Le Lavandou also has its own summer festival of the fishermen, called the Fête de Saint-Pierre, with its procession of sailors carrying the saint's statue to the sea to bless the waves, its Provençal mass,

and its nighttime *farandole*, or dance of brightly lit fishing boats in the port. Traditional tuna fishing in this region is commemorated by the Tuna Club and the Order of Taste-Thon with a great yearly event, the French tuna fishing championships.

Fresh tuna, neither the humblest nor most noble of the Mediterranean catch, certainly appears often on the menus of many contemporary Provençal chefs. Fresh anchovies as well as preserved ones are often used as a kind of condiment. Sardines are also a traditional staple of this coastline. Sea bass (*bar*, or more commonly *loup de mer*) are now raised in huge underwater beds and available all year round. Red mullet (*rouget barbet*) has long been a favorite (its liver considered a delicacy). Like sculpin (*rascasse*), indispensable in bouillabaisse, mullet has a strong flavor. Red sculpin or *chapon* is particularly prized by seafood chefs. Sea bream (*dorade* or *pageot rose*) lends itself well to grilling and baking or barbecue. And then there is the "poor man's lobster," the densely fleshed monkfish or anglerfish (*baudroie* or *lotte*), which is often judged the reigning Mediterranean fish for gastronomes.

Laurent Tarridec, chef and part owner of the Hôtel Les Roches, is a man of the sea, although he comes from Brittany and could hardly look less Provençal. Big, blond, curly haired, he strides across his dining room like a young Lancelot out of Arthurian romance. He traveled a good deal before finding his holy grail in Le Lavandou in 1988 and apprenticed in a long list of fine establishments, including La Bonne Auberge in Antibes, Prunier and Le Vivarois in Paris. Like his colleagues, Tarridec takes his vocation very seriously. The chef's aim is not, he says, to have fun, sometimes at the customer's expense, as did some adepts of nouvelle cuisine; on the contrary, the chef should create food that pleases and meets the needs of a contemporary public while maintaining ties with the heritage of the past. Provençal food? Seventeen million people in France speak with "the accent," he maintains; their culinary traditions must be respected and enjoyed.

Tarridec's version of Provençal food is the fisherman's and sailor's, open to influences from the other side of the inland sea. He uses spices skillfully to prepare fresh tuna with tabbouleh, for example. His treatment of the traditional Provençal stew or daube is grilled beef in the style of a "sailor's daube" with marrow bones and braised spring vegetables. In Tarridec's kitchen, country and mountain sources combine with the exotic: In a dessert, coconut sherbet accompanies a waffle spread with a very refined version of that old country recipe, bachelor's jam (*confiture de vieux garçon*), in which different fruits are layered in brandy and sugar as each matures throughout the summer. Tarridec's variant contains walnuts, blanched to just the right degree of soft crispness. Another backcountry inspiration is a dish of fillets, chops, and feet of milk-fed pork served lacquered with chestnuts, celery, and sage juice. A great range of breads is made on the premises.

This is not heavy fare, but it is still robust, with generous servings, beautifully but forcefully presented without frills and curlicues. Chocolates with coffee come on a beautiful chunk of granite or marble. Everything is solid and strong. Simplicity is a supreme elegance here: A slab of sole is served in a gently hot-peppered bouillon with an inventive, winter version of ratatouille—endives, fennel, sweet red peppers, carrots, leeks, and mushrooms carefully blended.

Tarridec's imagination is robust too, perhaps one of the most original on the coast. So is his sense of humor: The chef's *amuse-bouche* (an extra starter before the hors d'oeuvre, now de rigueur in any serious restaurant) may well be an uncomplicated, farm-fresh boiled egg—with caviar. One of his specialties is cold roast rabbit with burnt eggplant (*rôti de lapin froid aux aubergines brulés*). English words find their way onto the menu as well: Le "hot rock lobster" comes with curry and coconut milk and a tomato and apple compote. This is not surprising, since the Hôtel Les Roches has business connections in

England. As a result, it also has an extraordinary array of some fifty English and Irish cheeses. These still remain in the minority, however: Another platter has almost a hundred French cheeses.

Cheese, of course, is the domain of wine steward Philippe Gustin. He and Tarridec work closely together on a wine list as thick as a book. Gustin recently won the coveted Etiquette d'Or discerned by the Comité des Côtes de Provence for the best wine list of the region.

No wonder the Hôtel Les Roches has become a mecca for international connoisseurs of the good life. The following menu contains some very simple preparations, however: good seafood and a scrumptious dessert with local figs.

•

BARIGOULE OF GARDEN VEGETABLES WITH CLAMS
Barigoule de "tous les légumes" aux coquillages

Here is yet another version of the Provençal peasant dish, artichokes *barigoule*, now made with miniature vegetables. The technique of combining natural juices to make a sauce is typical of the new Provençal cuisine.
SERVES 4

THE BARIGOULE
4 baby artichokes
1 tablespoon fresh lemon juice
Salt, as needed
4 baby carrots or 2 medium-sized new carrots, halved
4 baby fennels or 1 medium-sized fennel, quartered
2 tablespoons olive oil
1 teaspoon coriander seeds
1 bay leaf
1 sprig fresh thyme
4 baby endives or 2 medium-sized endives

1/2 cup white wine
Freshly ground black pepper, to taste

1 pound clams in shells, well scrubbed
1 cup water
1 tablespoon chopped fresh coriander (cilantro)

To Prepare the Barigoule
Remove the outer leaves and stems from the artichokes, remove the chokes, and rub the exteriors of the artichokes with lemon juice. Bring a large saucepan of salted water to the boil Cook the carrots first, then the fennel separately, for 2 minutes each. Remove each from the boiling water with a slotted spoon. Plunge into a bowl of ice water, drain, and reserve.

In a medium-sized skillet, heat the olive oil over medium heat with the coriander seeds, bay leaf, and thyme. Add the artichokes and cook 5 minutes. Add the endives, fennels, carrots. white wine, salt, and pepper. Simmer until the vegetables have softened, about 15 to 20 minutes, depending on the size of the artichokes.

To Prepare the Clams and Serve
Put the clams in a large saucepan with 1 cup water. Bring to a boil, cover the pan, and remove from the heat. Leave for 5 minutes until the clams open, and discard any that do not open. Remove the remaining clams from their shells, carefully catching the liquor in a bowl.

Transfer the *barigoule* vegetables to 4 heated serving plates with a slotted spoon, reserving the cooking juices in the skillet. Arrange the clams on top of the vegetables. In a small bowl, combine the reserved clam and vegetable juices, season with salt and pepper, and spoon some over each plate. Sprinkle with the chopped coriander.

HERBED SARDINE FRITTERS WITH RED PEPPER PURÉE
Beignets legers de sardines aux feuilles aromatiques, purée de poivrons doux

A very simple recipe, with good color and texture contrasts. It takes some care in the timing of the deep-frying, however, since the sardines must be cooked only a few at a time.

SERVES 4

1 cup water

¹/₃ cup all-purpose flour

Salt and freshly ground black pepper, to taste

3 tablespoons olive oil

3 red bell peppers, roasted, peeled, and seeded (page 155) and cut into large pieces

1 to 1¹/₂ quarts peanut oil or safflower oil, for deep-frying

16 fresh sardines (4 to 5 inches long), boned and filleted

4 fresh sage leaves

4 fresh basil leaves

4 fresh flat-leaved parsley leaves

4 fresh curly parsley leaves

4 zucchini blossoms (optional), for garnish

In a medium-sized bowl, add the water to the flour gradually, stirring all the time to avoid lumps. Season and add I tablespoon of the olive oil. Set aside for 30 minutes.

Heat 2 tablespoons of the olive oil in a small skillet over low heat. Cook the red pepper pieces gently without allowing them to color, until soft (about 10 minutes). Transfer the mixture to a blender or food processor and purée to a thick consistency. Return mixture to pan and keep warm.

Heat the vegetable oil to 375°F in a deep-fryer or a large, heavy saucepan, until a I-inch cube of bread browns evenly in I minute.

Dip the sardines into the fritter batter to coat evenly, I or 2 at a time. Fry them, a few at a time, in the hot oil until golden brown, drain on paper towels, transfer to a platter, salt immediately, and keep warm. When all the fish are cooked, dip the herb leaves and zucchini blossoms, if using, individually in the remaining fritter batter and fry in the same manner until golden, for just a few seconds.

Arrange the sardines on each of 4 plates with the puréed peppers. Decorate with the fried herb leaves and zucchini blossoms, if desired.

•

STEWED FIGS WITH MUSCAT WINE AND FENNEL
Grosses figues mauves au Beaumes-de-Venise, infusion de fenouil

Herbal infusions commonly contribute to the preparation of everything from soup to dessert in the new Provençal cuisine. Tarridec uses a sweet, highly aromatic muscat wine from Baumes-de-Venise, a charming village northeast of Avignon. Another sweet dessert wine could be substituted. Note that this compote should be refrigerated overnight for best results.
SERVES 4

2¹/₂ cups muscat or other syrupy, aromatic dessert wine
¹/₂ cup strongly flavored honey
¹/₂ teaspoon fennel seeds
2 sprigs dried fennel twigs (optional)
1 pound large fresh purple figs, stems removed
Vanilla ice cream (store-bought or page 155), for garnish
Slices of spice cake or gingerbread (optional), for accompaniment

In a medium-sized saucepan, combine the wine, honey, fennel seeds, and dried fennel, if using. Bring to a boil, add the figs, and simmer until soft but still holding their shape, about 20 minutes. Using a slotted spoon, transfer the figs to a bowl, reserving the cooking liquid in the pan. Return the pan to high heat, bring to a boil, and reduce the juices by half. Pour over the figs, cover, and refrigerate overnight.

To serve, arrange the figs and liquid in shallow bowls with a scoop of vanilla ice cream and a slice of spice cake or gingerbread, if desired.

Food for Artists

in Saint-Tropez

MENU

FRESH TUNA AND SWEET PEPPER TERRINE
Filets de thon frais, poivrons verts et rouges
marinés à l'olive, légumes croquants

HERBED STEAKS WITH ANCHOVY, RED WINE,
AND OLIVE SAUCE
Tournedos rôtis façon "totti," sauce vin rouge à l'olive

A PALETTE OF PROVENÇAL VEGETABLES
Artichauts barigoule, pagret de tomates,
râpée de pommes

PEACH AND RASPBERRY MOUSSE WITH PASSION
FRUIT SAUCE AND STRAWBERRY COULIS
Chaud-froid de fruits rouges au parfum de pêche blanche,
jus de fruits de la passion, coulis de fraises
et vin rouge

FRANCIS CARDAILLAC   *Restaurant L'Olivier at La Bastide de Saint-Tropez*   SAINT-TROPEZ

Saint-Tropez is one of those magic sites set between wild, unspoiled hills and the vast blue sea that attracts cosmopolitans of every description. Here they rub shoulders with fishermen and peasants—even today, as proved by recent litigation. When film star Brigitte Bardot brought suit against a local shepherd for cruelty to animals, newspaper readers were surprised to learn that shepherds still survive in the outskirts of such a glamorous community. But indeed, flocks do still graze on the rugged peninsula south of the town, among vineyards which have evolved from producing rustic rosés to subtle wines of all colors. Fishermen still take out their picturesque boats for tuna and sardines and sell their catches on the port—even if most moorage now belongs to opulent yachts or the streamlined beauties that partake in world-famous sailboat races.

Noted writer Colette reigned over an earlier community of artists. Often they all simply improvised potlucks. Everything was spontaneous and relaxed. The artists at Saint-Tropez deliberately avoided the snobbery and pretention of coastal resorts further east.

This is still the spirit of Saint-Tropez today, and a number of talented chefs cater to its public of festive cosmopolitans. One of the best is Francis Cardaillac, who presides over the restaurant L'Olivier at the hotel called La Bastide de Saint-Tropez. He combines adventure and artistry in the best Saint-Tropez tradition.

Colette and her cronies of the late twenties were not the first artists to discover Saint-Tropez's special atmosphere. The fauve and pointillist painters had arrived already before World War I. Always there was color—bright, glad, gay. In 1892, painter Paul Signac arrived in Saint-Tropez on his boat, the *Olympia*. He exclaimed, "I have just discovered happiness," and settled down for years of fruitful production. In 1905, Matisse was moved by the bay of Saint-Tropez to create his famous picture *Luxe, Calme et Volupté*, In 1908, the young

painter André Dunoyer de Segonzac observed the much older Signac transforming a colorful array of boats and sails into canvases covered with spots of pure, brilliant color. He commented: "How nice! Nature is giving the pointillist painters their pictures already composed!" Colette herself left numerous word pictures of this "little Mediterranean port, with its tuna boats, its flat houses painted in tones of candy pink, lavender blue, linden green, its streets where float the odors of melon peel, nougat, and sea urchins."

Francis Cardaillac has come to appreciate, and even to exemplify, the Saint-Tropez style. He began life as a landlubber, however, in the rich gastronomic region of southwest France, near Agen. There his parents had a country inn, where his mother was cook.

Cardaillac longed to travel and was already setting sail for distant horizons when his mother fell ill. A dutiful son, he took over her kitchen. And then he fell in love—with cooking and, more specifically, with *"la cuisine des femmes."* He defines this as skillful improvisation and subtle invention ("a bit of lard here, a bit of chocolate there"), respect for seasonal production, and the desire to give pleasure.

Although master of his own restaurant by the age of twenty-one, Cardaillac did finally set sail, or rather took flight, for the United States, where he worked as chef for a series of celebrities. In 1988, he returned as chef de cuisine to the Restaurant L'Olivier at La Bastide de Saint-Tropez.

This wonderful, old, faded-pink villa, decked with brilliant bougainvillea ("floral lava," says Colette) has been extended by a series of independent units, linked by patios, steps, trellises, and splendidly architectural exotic plantations around the large pool. Discretion is the byword at the hotel—as many celebrities have come to appreciate. Informality reigns: Residents may eat where they please—on their own veranda, by the pool, or in the dining room. The latter, thanks to a system of glass partitions, can be as much indoors or outdoors as the season allows, but is always sheltered by the canopies of ancient olive trees. The pool is not visible from the raised dining terrace, but its overflow is audible as a gentle, cooling murmur.

Francis Cardaillac regulates his restaurant with meticulous care; even the timing of service to each table is carefully controlled. No one element should dominate intrusively, he feels, not the décor, nor the service, nor the food. In this aim, however, he fails, for the food is definitely outstanding.

Each dish is an adventure, each has its own itinerary, and each diner follows his or her own path. Breaking with the usual practice in which the main elements are presented in the center of the plate, with garnishes and sauces spooned over or arranged on the outside edges, Cardaillac sets out his food asymmetrically. If you go in one direction, you come upon a stuffed cauliflower floret; in another, a sprinkling of sweet paprika, which you can blend with other elements as you alone decide. You are the artist, the plate is your palette, and each dish is a picture. Cardaillac often arranges spices around the outer edge, so that individual mixtures are possible. Perhaps the surest sign of Cardaillac's being happy in Saint-Tropez is his exuberant display of color. It might be a confetti of red and green peppers, paprika, and herbs or a pattern of tiny vegetables, each with its own stuffing or garnish.

Even a dessert hides a frozen, liqueur-soaked fig in the heart of a walnut custard, and you fall upon it as on hidden treasure. Thus there is a fanciful complicity between cook and diner, the former sharing his delight with the latter as the meal progresses.

The following menu is complex, as each dish is composed of several independent preparations to be assembled before serving. Each individual step, however, is simple. And as is usually the case in the new style, these recipes offer a whole panoply of ideas and techniques, which can be taken separately and used singly, or adapted elsewhere.

•

FRESH TUNA
AND SWEET PEPPER TERRINE
Filets de thon frais, poivrons verts et rouges marinés à l'olive, légumes croquants

This is one of Cardaillac's prettiest recipes, using his usual wide variety of vegetables, herbs, and spices. A good example of the itinerary-on-the-plate idea, thanks to their artful arrangement. If preferred, however, the chopped herbs could be added to the terrine when it is layered. Some care must be taken in removing the slices from the dish and a very sharp knife is recommended. If, however, the terrine still does not hold together in even slices, it can be just as pretty and taste just as good in a looser arrangement in the center of the plate. To allow for adequate marination and chilling, begin this recipe two days before serving.

SERVES 6

THE TERRINE
2 pounds fresh tuna fillet
About 1 pound sea salt, as needed
1¼ pounds each red and green bell peppers, roasted, peeled, seeded, and halved (page 155)
1 cup olive oil plus 1 tablespoon for greasing pan
4 cloves garlic, unpeeled and crushed
2 pounds ripe tomatoes, peeled, seeded, and finely diced
1 teaspoon coriander seeds
Salt and freshly ground black pepper, to taste
4 ounces sun-dried tomatoes in oil, drained and chopped

THE VEGETABLE GARNISH
12 mini-carrots or 6 baby carrots, peeled
6 mini-fennels or 1 regular-sized fennel, tough outer leaves removed, cut into 6 equal pieces
12 green onions, trimmed
¼ cup balsamic vinegar
3 tablespoons chopped mixed fresh herbs (tarragon, basil, dill)
2 ounces pickled nasturtium buds or regular capers in vinegar
3 tablespoons coarse sea salt, for garnish

To Prepare the Terrine

Remove the skin and the central bones from the tuna and cut into strips, removing any tough bits. Sprinkle generously with 3 to 4 handfuls sea salt, rubbing it into the fish and coating well. Set aside for at least 30 minutes. Then rinse thoroughly and dry on paper towels.

Put the tuna and the peppers in a deep bowl just large enough to hold them with the olive oil and crushed garlic cloves. Turn so that all pieces are evenly coated with oil. Cover and marinate at least 12 hours in the refrigerator.

Strain the tuna and the peppers into a bowl, reserving the oil, juices, and garlic. Peel 2 of the garlic cloves from the marinade and chop very fine. In a medium-sized bowl, mix the chopped garlic with the tomato dice and coriander seeds. Season with salt and pepper and set aside.

Lightly brush with olive oil an $8^{1}/_{2} \times 4^{1}/_{2} \times 3^{1}/_{2}$-inch glass loaf pan or a 6-cup terrine. Wrap half the tuna strips in pieces of red pepper, the other half in pieces of green pepper. Place the stuffed red peppers in the bottom of the terrine and spread between and over them half the fresh tomato mixture. Layer all the dried tomatoes on top, then add another layer of tomato dice. Top with the tuna pieces wrapped in green peppers. Lay a piece of plastic wrap over the peppers and place on top a brick wrapped in plastic wrap or a board smaller than the dish, weighted with several pounds of canned goods. Chill for at least 6 hours.

To Garnish and Serve

If using mini-vegetables, cut the carrots in half and the fennels in quarters lengthwise. If using regular vegetables, cut baby carrots in quarters lengthwise, and the fennel in long strips. Cut the green onions in quarters lengthwise, keeping part of the green.

Prepare a vinaigrette in a small bowl by beating into the balsamic vinegar $1^{1}/_{2}$ cups of the reserved oil and juices from the marinade. Adjust the seasoning.

To serve, cut the terrine in the dish with a very sharp knife into 6 even slices and place a slice in the center of each of 6 plates. In a pretty manner, arrange the carrots, fennel, and onion strips in a fan shape on each side of each terrine slice. Complete the circle with the chopped herbs and the nasturtium buds. Sprinkle the vinaigrette over all, along with coarse salt. Cover loosely with plastic wrap and chill before serving.

•

HERBED STEAKS WITH ANCHOVY, RED WINE, AND OLIVE SAUCE
Tournedos rôtis façon "totti," sauce vin rouge à l'olive

Anchovy sauce served with steak is an old Niçois tradition, and, much to the surprise of the neophyte, is absolutely delicious. Cardaillac likes to brown the steaks in duck fat but finds blander oils quite acceptable.
SERVES 6

30 pitted black olives
2 cloves garlic, minced
1 teaspoon chopped fresh marjoram
$^{1}/_{2}$ cup olive oil
6 anchovy fillets in oil, drained
Salt and freshly ground black pepper, to taste
1 tablespoon peanut oil or safflower oil
6 small fillets of beef (about 6 ounces each)
2 cups full-bodied red wine
2 tablespoons butter
A Palette of Provençal Vegetables (following),
*   for accompaniment*
Pitted black olives and marjoram sprigs, for garnish

Preheat the broiler. In a blender or food processor, purée together 15 black olives with the garlic, marjoram, olive oil, and anchovy fillets to make a thick cream. Season with salt and pepper and set aside.

In a large, heavy-bottomed skillet, heat the peanut oil over high heat and sear the steaks, without salt or pepper, turning once, 1 to 2 minutes on each side. When well browned but still raw inside, remove them from the pan and set them in an ovenproof dish just large enough to hold them. Spread their tops generously with the anchovy and olive mixture, reserving a tablespoon for the sauce. Place under the broiler until a light crust forms and the meat has reached desired doneness, 3 to 7 minutes.

While the meat cooks, prepare the sauce: With a spoon, remove any fat from the skillet in which the meat was browned. Add the red wine, place over high heat, and reduce by half, scraping to pick up any brown bits from the bottom of the skillet.

In a blender or food processor, purée the butter with the remaining 15 pitted olives. Stir into the reduced wine a few teaspoons of this olive butter along with the reserved tablespoon of the anchovy preparation. Remove from the heat and adjust the seasoning. The sauce must not boil once these additions are made.

On each of 6 warmed serving plates, place a slice of potato cake and put a steak on top. On the side, arrange the cold tomato relish, and in the center of each small heap, place a dollop of the *barigoule*. Spoon some of the anchovy sauce around in a decorative manner, and serve the rest separately. Decorate each plate further with a few olives and sprigs of marjoram, if desired. Using a pepper mill, grind a small heap of pepper on the edge of each plate, so that each person may use as much as he or she chooses.

A PALETTE
OF PROVENÇAL VEGETABLES
Artichauts barigoule, pagret de tomates, râpée de pommes

The peasant *barigoule* vegetable medley appears here in yet another version. The tomato relish, or *pagret*, also belongs to old Niçois cuisine. Along with the potato cake, it adds a great deal to the skillful blend of textures and temperatures combined here, as well as flavors. But of course each of these vegetables could be served separately on other occasions.

SERVES 6

THE BARIGOULE

6 baby artichokes, chokes removed
6 tablespoons olive oil
1 thick slice bacon or salt pork (about 2 ounces), diced and blanched 3 seconds in boiling water
3 medium-sized carrots, cut into thin strips
2 medium-sized onions, cut into thin rounds
1/2 cup white wine
1 sprig fresh thyme
2 cloves garlic, minced
2 strips orange zest
Salt and freshly ground black pepper, to taste

THE PAGRET OF TOMATOES

1/4 teaspoon prepared mustard
1 1/2 tablespoons wine vinegar
5 tablespoons olive oil
2 tablespoons chopped fresh basil
2 tablespoons chopped fresh parsley
1 clove garlic, minced
3 ripe tomatoes (about 1 pound), peeled, seeded, and finely diced
Salt and freshly ground black pepper, to taste

THE POTATO CAKES

1/2 stick (4 tablespoons) butter
1 pound potatoes, peeled and coarsely grated
Salt and freshly ground black pepper, to taste
1 tablespoon chopped, fresh, mixed herbs (tarragon, chives, parsley)

To Prepare the Barigoule

Preheat the oven to 350°F. Remove the outside leaves of the artichokes and trim the bottoms to give them a neat shape. Heat 2 tablespoons olive oil in a medium-sized skillet that can go into the oven or in a flameproof casserole over medium-high heat. Add the diced bacon or salt pork and let it brown lightly, 3 to 4 minutes. Add the carrots and cook a few minutes, then the onions for a few minutes more, then the artichokes. When all have turned golden, add the white wine, thyme, remaining 4 tablespoons of the olive oil, garlic, and orange zest. Season with salt and pepper. Transfer to the oven and bake until the mixture reduces to a thick mass and all the vegetables are cooked through, about 30 minutes, depending on the size of the artichokes.

To Prepare the Tomato Pagret

In a medium-sized salad bowl, combine all the *pagret* ingredients. Mix gently and adjust the seasoning.

To Prepare the Potato Cakes

In a medium-sized, nonstick skillet, heat the butter over medium-high heat. Add the potatoes, season with salt and pepper, and flatten them with a spatula. Cook until golden and firm on the bottom, about 10 minutes. Turn the potato cake gently and let it brown until cooked through, about 10 minutes more. Carefully remove it from the skillet to a plate covered with paper towels, to absorb any excess fat. Sprinkle over it the chopped fresh herbs, and keep warm.

PEACH AND RASPBERRY MOUSSE WITH PASSION FRUIT SAUCE AND STRAWBERRY COULIS

*Chaud-froid de fruits rouges au parfum
de pêche blanche, jus de fruits de la passion,
coulis de fraises et vin rouge*

Ice cream and fruit combinations are typical of the new desserts, and hark back to Escoffier's legendary, super-simple *pêche Melba* (vanilla ice cream with peach halves and raspberry purée). Although Cardaillac uses passion fruit sherbet for a sauce here, any other peferred fruit flavor which will provide a color and flavor contrast to the strawberry-wine sauce may be substituted.
SERVES 6

THE MOUSSE
1/2 pint good quality raspberry sherbet
6 tablespoons sugar
4 eggs, separated
1 1/2 tablespoons peach liqueur

THE SAUCES
1/2 pint good quality passion fruit sherbet
3 cups full-bodied red wine
1 cinnamon stick
1 pint strawberries
1/2 cup sugar

THE GARNISH
3 tablespoons dark brown sugar
1/2 cup strawberries, hulled
1/2 cup raspberries
1/2 cup black currants or other seasonal fruit,
  prepared for eating
Fresh mint sprigs

To Prepare the Mousse

Divide the raspberry sherbet into 6 small scoops and set on a plate in the freezer while preparing the mousse, so that they are readily available.

In a medium-sized bowl, add 3 tablespoons sugar to the egg whites and beat them until stiff peaks form. In a large bowl, add 3 tablespoons sugar to the yolks and beat them until lemon colored. Stir the peach liqueur into the yolk mixture. Gently fold in the whites.

Distribute half this mousse into 6 individual ramekins. Place a ball of raspberry sherbet in the center of each and cover with the remaining mousse. Place the ramekins on a plate or cookie sheet, cover with plastic wrap, and put in the freezer for 2 hours.

To Prepare the Sauces

Set the passion-fruit or other sherbet to melt in a small bowl and strain when melted. Put the wine in a medium-sized saucepan with the cinnamon stick, and simmer it until reduced to about 3/4 cup. Add the wine to the strawberries and sugar in a blender or food processor and purée. (Or push through a sieve.) You should have two smooth sauces.

To Assemble the Dessert

Preheat the broiler. Take the mousses from the freezer. Unmold each onto a heatproof plate. Sprinkle 1/2 tablespoon dark brown sugar on the top of each mousse. Dribble the strawberry sauce on one side, the passion fruit sauce on the other, to make a pretty pattern. Place under the broiler for just a few seconds, until the sugar melts and turns golden. Serve immediately, surrounded by the fresh fruit and mint sprigs, decoratively arranged.

The Golden Riviera

MENU

RED MULLET WITH BASIL BRANDADE
Filets de rouget en brandade à l'huile d'olive

FILLET OF VEAL WITH CITRUS BUTTER
Mignons de veau au beurre d'agrumes

CANDIED-FENNEL TART
WITH STAR ANISE ICE CREAM
Tarte au fenouil confit, glace à l'anis étoilé

JEAN-CLAUDE GUILLON   *Grand Hôtel du Cap-Ferrat*   SAINT-JEAN-CAP-FERRAT

The French Riviera is a phenomenon unique in Europe, perhaps in the world. The vagaries of history turned this little stretch of coastline into a melting pot for royalty, artists and writers, painters, sculptors, dancers, cinema actors, and musicians of all nations, the very rich and famous, and those less rich, who, for reasons of their own, could not live at home. A sunny place for shady people, as Somerset Maugham called it. The Riviera has also been a speedy place, and owed much of its good fortune to the development first of the railroad, then of the automobile.

The opulent "palace" hotels of the Riviera were built between 1900 and World War I to accommodate the new flood of affluent travelers arriving by rail and road—the Negresco in Nice, the Hôtel de Paris in Monaco, the Carleton in Cannes among them. The latter's twin cupolas are said to have been modeled after the splendid breasts of the influential courtesan known as La Belle Otéro, whose lovers included four kings and a Vanderbilt. By 1900, local train connections made possible a new extravagance in interurban dining: Visitors stopping in more sedate Cannes would send their valets, maids, and gala dress clothes to Monaco's Hôtel de Paris in the morning by the local train. They would follow themselves later in the afternoon, spend two hours dressing for a dinner in the hotel's restaurant, then finish the evening at the casino.

Indeed, the Hôtel de Paris' fashionable restaurant had a curious impact on belle epoque dining customs: Respectable women, who would never dream of dining out in Paris, could be seen in this establishment, since Monaco was considered a resort like the spa towns. The

ladies might well run into male acquaintances traveling incognito in the company of demimondaines. But this problem was solved by a simple rule of cosmopolitan etiquette: The society women simply affected not to recognize the men, while carefully observing their companions' splendor.

Crêpes Suzette were invented at the Hôtel de Paris, baptized by the Prince of Wales (later Edward VIII) in honor of a passing companion after a clumsy waiter accidentally set fire to the dessert.

More modest restaurants existed, even in Monte Carlo, but sometimes attracted the same cosmopolitan patronage. American newspaper magnate James Gould Bennett (who sent Stanley into Africa to look for Livingstone) ate regularly in a small restaurant whose mutton chops he particularly appreciated. On one occasion he found all the best tables on the terrace occupied. Outraged, Bennett immediately bought the restaurant for some $40,000, and when he finally received his mutton chops, gave the deed to the waiter as a tip. The lucky recipient of this largess was thus able to start his own, long restaurant career, under the name Ciro's.

Several famous "palace" hotels of the Riviera were built not in cities but on the rocky promontories jutting out into the Mediterranean. The Grand Hôtel of Saint-Jean-Cap-Ferrat, where chef Jean-Claude Guillon presides today, sits at the very tip of the headland, plunging into the sea, not far from Somerset Maugham's legendary Villa Mauresque. The hotel was conceived on the grand scale indeed, but always remained more discrete than its counterparts like the Hôtel du Cap south of Antibes, no doubt because the Grand Hotel frequently housed royalty and royal relatives—equally demanding customers but who (in those days at least) avoided newspaper exposure. Today Guillon welcomes other national leaders, such as French politician Raymond Barre, who has a house nearby.

The glitz and glitter of the golden Riviera survived two major world wars. When the Allies bombed parts of

this coast in 1944, prior to landing, a *New York Times* correspondent specifically asked that the Carlton be spared because it was the best hotel in the world. Aly Khan was among the British officers who liberated the Carlton shortly afterwards and commented: "I was received by the management there as if I had never been away." The Negresco, during the liberation, offered full luxury service to American officers—if they would provide the food.

The Côte d'Azur heritage is curious indeed, and a difficult one for contemporaries to assume. What sort of food was served to this glamorous public, and does it have anything to offer as a model for today's Riviera chefs? Escoffier was one of the first great cooks for the jet-setting public of the coast, and he is still highly regarded by today's younger generation. The house he was born in near Nice has become a delightful small museum, the Fondation Escoffier, in Villeneuve-Loubet. The great chef got his start at the Grand Hôtel in Monte Carlo. But in spite of roots deep in the local *terroir*, he obviously adjusted his cuisine to suit the tastes of his capricious, cosmopolitan, and worldly public. And indeed, he made his reputation on his work not in Provence, but in Paris and London.

On the whole, the French Riviera in its golden age had little to offer serious gastronomes. Food writer Waverley Root judged as late as the 1960s that "these cosmopolitan vacation centers cater to an international population, and provide it with the international standarized hotel cuisine. The majority of the restaurants' customers have no roots there and provide no encouragement for regional cooking—and their presence corrupts the natives."

The French gastronomic establishment, moreover, for decades looked askance at hotel restaurants, wherever they might be. How could a chef be expected to concentrate on his art if he had to cater to tennis players, actresses, politicians?—people whose reasons for being in his dining room had nothing to do with the quality of the meal or who, at the very most, came merely for the glitter of his reputation.

Today, all this has changed. There are currently more starred and touted restaurants on the Riviera than in any other French province. And many excellent contemporary chefs now work in hotels. The explanations for this dramatic reversal are diverse: Paradoxically it partly results from the current fashion for the *terroir* and rural roots. Today's cosmopolitan Riviera public actually spends vast fortunes (though perhaps a bit less vast than in the belle epoque) pursuing a dream of simple, country life in various forms. Many elaborate backcountry villa gardens now include a vegetable plot, and their owners are proud of serving olive oil pressed from fruit grown

on the property. This public now expects country-inspired cuisine, even in glamorous hotel settings.

Partly, too, the change results from the new status of chefs as stars. Escoffier laid the groundwork for this change of status, and today the Hôtel de Paris is famous above all for the sophisticated "country cooking" of star chef Alain Ducasse.

Hotel managements have also become much more imaginative in meeting the gastronomic expectations of one part of their public, while satisfying the more mundane needs of the rest. Jean-Claude Guillon at the Grand Hôtel on Saint-Jean-Cap-Ferrat has devised a clever series of menus around basic winter and summer themes for his customers, who may eat twice a day in his dining room. This allows seasonal and marketing variation and choice for everyone's tastes. There are always four appetizers, four fish, and four meat dishes on the set menu, including both classics and lighter food like roast lamb and grilled turbot.

Guillon has worked for the same establishment for the last twenty-two years and loves it. Much like Escoffier, he has always stayed with resort hotels, by the Mediterranean in the summer, in Switzerland in winter. New owners, who took over the hotel in 1980, were wise enough to give him carte blanche with the restaurant, and by 1986 he had acquired the first Michelin star.

Guillon's jovial, festive cuisine appeals today both to the varied and international clientele of the hotel and to local residents (the mayor of Saint-Jean-Cap-Ferrat regularly entertains here). His cooking also pleases his fellow chefs, who come to dine and even hold here their children's weddings. Guillon meets and gossips with his colleagues twice a week at Nice's lovely open-air market on the Cours Saleya.

Like most of the young chefs, Guillon was brought up on country cooking. But his grandmother, cook for the owners of a particularly elegant château in Burgundy, and his parents, professional caterers, had already learned to adapt the *terroir* to cosmopolitan tastes. Like the other chefs today, he regards traditional Provençal food as an inspiration for personal innovation. But in his case, he feels it would also be too rustic for his particular clientele. He always serves his fish filleted, explaining: "Many of my clients have never seen a fish whole." His original creations are inspired by the produce of the region, but on the Riviera he can get practically anything in the world.

In 1990, the Grand Hôtel began a new life, as part of the Bel Air network. This is jet-set living indeed, for the Cap-Ferrat property now becomes the sister hotel of the Bel Air in Los Angeles. Each keeps its special character, however: The Riviera hotel sits among its sixteen acres of pinewoods and gardens, dramatically overlooking the sea. Indeed, its swimming pool (reached by a private funicular) juts out right over the waves, backed by a whole hillside of brilliantly colored, exotic rockery plants. But the heart of the hotel remains its wonderful dining terrace, set on a platform under ancient umbrella pines.

The following menu is elegant but simple. The dishes require very few ingredients, but these must be of excellent quality.

RED MULLET
WITH BASIL BRANDADE
Filets de rouget en brandade à l'huile d'olive

Inspired by the traditional country dish of Nîmes, a gratin of salt cod and mashed potatoes called *brandade*, this version is much faster to prepare. Sautéed fish fillets are simply garnished (not baked) with olive-oil enriched, roughly mashed potatoes. Some chefs still add milk when making mashed potatoes with olive oil, to keep the mix lighter, but Guillon prefers the simpler version. His sauce, in keeping with today's trends, makes use of trimmings to produce a broth that is reduced and enriched just before serving. And although he uses the French *rouget* (red mullet), red snapper or Hawaiian goatfish may be substituted for similar flavor. Be sure to ask the fishmonger for bones for the stock.

SERVES 4

8 red mullet fillets (2 to 3 ounces each), skin intact,
   bones of 2 fish reserved for making stock
1/2 cup white wine
2 cups water
1 small shallot, minced
Salt and freshly ground black pepper, to taste
1 1/2 pounds potatoes, peeled and cooked until tender
About 1 1/2 cups olive oil, as needed
1 stick (1/4 pound) butter
1/2 clove garlic, chopped, or more, to taste
1 cup chopped fresh basil plus 4 leaves, for garnish

Rinse fish fillets and pat dry. Put the 2 fish carcasses, white wine, water, shallot, salt, and pepper in a large saucepan and bring to a boil. Reduce the heat and simmer uncovered about 15 minutes. Strain into a small saucepan and set aside; there should be about 1 1/2 cups liquid left.

To prepare the mashed potatoes, crush the cooked and drained potatoes with a fork or potato masher. Beat in 1/4 cup olive oil, 6 tablespoons of the reserved fish broth, then more oil if desired. Season with salt and pepper and keep warm.

To prepare the sauce, boil down the remaining fish broth until it is reduced to about 1/2 cup. Lower the heat, and add the butter, bit by bit, to the hot liquid, beating all the while, without boiling. Then slowly beat in 1 scant cup olive oil, whisking to make a thickened sauce. Add the minced garlic. Strain and keep warm. Add the chopped basil just before serving so that it stays green.

In a nonstick skillet, heat the remaining 1 tablespoon olive oil over medium-high heat. Sauté the fish fillets skin side down, without turning, until the skin is nicely browned and the fillets are cooked through (4 to 10 minutes). Remove the fillets to paper toweling to remove any excess fat. Transfer to a platter and keep warm.

On each of 4 warmed serving plates, form 2 flat circles of potato purée. Spoon over a little of the basil sauce. Gently arrange the fish fillets, skin side up, on the potatoes and decorate with the remaining basil leaves. Serve the rest of the sauce separately.

•

FILLET OF VEAL
WITH CITRUS BUTTER
Mignons de veau au beurre d'agrumes

Again, Guillon proposes a fast and simple, last-minute preparation which is fun and original. The dish could also be made with thinly sliced pork tenderloin. The citrus blend is a happy echo of Riviera landscapes where, already in the eighteenth century, English novelist Tobias Smollett admired "gardens full of green trees loaded with oranges, lemons, citrons, and bergomots, which make a delightful appearance . . ." The chef recommends a red wine for this dish to accommodate the citrus sauce. Broccoli, carrots, or green beans would be good accompaniments as all have colors, textures, and flavors that complement the citrus.

SERVES 4

2 oranges
1 lemon
1 pink grapefruit
1 stick (1/4 pound) butter
1 tablespoon peanut or safflower oil
1 1/2 pounds veal tenderloin, trimmed and cut into
    12 equal pieces
Salt and freshly ground black pepper, to taste

Preheat the oven to 300°F. Peel the oranges, lemon, and grapefruit over a bowl to catch the juice as you work. Separate the segments, removing all white skin, still saving the juice. Put the segments in a heatproof bowl and warm them in the oven without cooking them, 5 to 10 minutes.

Heat 2 tablespoons of the butter and the peanut oil in a large skillet over medium-high heat. Sauté the veal slices, turning once, until nicely browned and cooked through, 7 to 10 minutes depending on thickness. Season with salt and pepper. Remove the pan from the heat. With a slotted spoon, remove the veal to a warm plate. Use paper toweling to absorb any excess fat. Cover with a second plate turned upside down, to keep it warm.

Return the skillet to the burner and warm over medium-high heat. Add the citrus juices to the pan and scrape the brown bits from the bottom. Beat in the remaining 6 tablespoons of the butter, bit by bit, to thicken the sauce.

Arrange 3 veal pieces in a star shape on each of 4 plates with the warm citrus segments around them. Strain the sauce and spoon over the meat. Serve immediately.

CANDIED-FENNEL TART WITH STAR ANISE ICE CREAM
Tarte au fenouil confit, glace à l'anis étoilé

This delicious and unusual creation blends two variants on licorice flavor—fennel and star anise. Not really a tart as such, this dessert simply layers pastry rounds, custard cream, and the fennel garnish. Be sure to use the decorative Chinese star anise (as the French have for centuries), not aniseed. Make the ice cream at least four hours before serving.

SERVES 4

THE ANISE ICE CREAM
2 1/2 cups milk
2 1/2 cups heavy cream
1/4 cup granulated white sugar
1 teaspoon star anise
6 egg yolks

THE FENNEL TARTS
3 cups sugar syrup (store-bought or page 155)
1 pound fennel, tough outer leaves removed,
    cut into fine dice
1/2 cup thick custard cream (store-bought or
    page 154)
12 ounces puff pastry cut into four 4-inch circles
    1/8 inch thick (store-bought or page 153)
1/3 cup powdered sugar

Fresh fennel sprigs, for garnish

To Prepare the Ice Cream
In a small saucepan, combine the milk, cream, and sugar over medium heat and bring just to the boiling point. Add the star anise and let it infuse for 2 hours.

Strain the milk mixture into another saucepan, rinse

off the anise, and set aside. In a large bowl, beat the egg yolks. Over medium heat, bring the milk mixture just to the boiling point and pour it little by little over the yolks in the bowl, stirring constantly to blend well. Return the contents of the bowl to the saucepan and cook over low heat until it thickens slightly. Do not allow it to boil. Strain the cream and freeze in an ice-cream maker according to the manufacturer's directions.

To Prepare the Tarts

Preheat the oven to 475°F. In a large saucepan over medium heat, bring the sugar syrup to a boil and add the fennel, bit by bit, stirring. Cook at a slow boil until the fennel is translucent and candied, about 25 minutes. Remove it from the syrup with a slotted spoon and reserve.

Spread 2 tablespoons custard cream on each pastry round. Arrange the candied fennel on top, in an even layer. Bake until the pastry is cooked, about 15 minutes. Sprinkle with powdered sugar and leave 2 more minutes in the oven.

To Assemble the Dessert

On each plate, place a fennel tart and 2 small scoops of ice cream. Decorate with the reserved star anise and sprigs of fresh fennel.

JEAN-CLAUDE GUILLON

The Country Connoisseur

MENU

FISH WITH GREEN ONION BROTH
Poisson au jus d'oignon nouveau

ROAST SQUAB WITH CUMIN-SPICED, OLIVE
POLENTA, BRAISED CARROTS, AND FAVA BEANS
*Pigeon à la polente d'olive au cumin avec sa
barigoule de carottes aux fevettes*

ORANGE SORBET WITH BASIL SAUCE
Sorbet à l'orange sauce basilic

JACQUES CHIBOIS   *La Bastide de Saint-Antoine*   GRASSE

Jacques Maximin, for many years the star chef of Nice's glamorous Hôtel Negresco, once claimed that his long-term aim was to become a simple innkeeper in the hills behind Nice. How many chefs have aspired to having such a place of their own? An idyllic spot for good living and good eating, where the cook may share his pleasures and enthusiasms with an appreciative public.

Jacques Chibois has quietly accomplished that goal. His Bastide de Saint-Antoine, set on a peaceful hillside south of Grasse, opened its doors in June 1995.

When Chibois was awarded a prize in 1991 as the most talented chef in France under forty-five years of age, he was still working for a prestigious "palace" hotel. During the fourteen years that he spent in the city of Cannes, he presided like a virtuoso conductor over the Gray d'Albion hotel's five restaurants, of which the Royal Gray earned him his culinary reputation. He was always gracious, organized, inventive in spite of his heavy responsibilities—sometimes eighteen hundred meals to serve daily. His slight figure could be seen zigzagging through the lobby, alighting here and there to greet the faithful (who ranged from the old families of Cannes to the stars of its film festival). He became known for an impeccable courtesy, an attentive ear, an intelligent look, and a broad, highly infectious cherub's grin.

But if, as poet Paul Valéry says, genius means biding your time, then Jacques Chibois definitely counts as a genius! He spent these years in Cannes looking for the perfect place and finally unearthed one of the Riviera's greatest treasures: a completely unspoiled old property, an ocher-colored *bastide* set among some four hundred ancient olive trees and tall cypress sentinels. Such terraced slopes around the city of Grasse have astonished and delighted travelers for centuries with their exuberant fields of flowers grown for the perfume factories. Some of France's most elegant old domains and gardens are tucked away in these hills. Jacques Chibois, finally, has left city glamor behind. He has moved to the country.

He came, originally, from the country. Chibois' family were small farmers in the Limousin, in southwest France. He grew up close to the land—keeping the geese, feeding the family pig. His first model in cooking was his mother, who ran a small restaurant and imbued in him the ideal of cuisine as an expression of festivity, gaiety, and generosity. In fact, Chibois is one of several young chefs to praise the traditions and practices of women's cooking: the capacity to be creative with very little, and the desire to give pleasure to loved ones. He much admires the many small restaurants run by women in the United States, feeling that it is women cooks who preserve the taste heritage of a country.

But Chibois does not wax sentimental, either about his grass roots or motherhood. He knows that culinary art, like any other, needs patrons who are both educated and willing to pay for quality. The best eggs will be eaten either on the farm itself or in a restaurant whose chef takes the trouble and expense to seek them out and bring them, fast and fresh, to his table. Chibois' ideal is a kind of rustic refinement. His Riviera is one of country resources transformed (though always respected) by the magician chef into food for cosmopolitan connoisseurs. Simplicity is the ultimate sophistication—without taking itself too seriously.

Elizabeth David once wrote an essay in praise of "the art of leaving well alone," which she considered the prerequisite of any first-class meal on any level whatsoever. Jacques Chibois has mastered this art. His sublime *sar à la Provençale* is fish poached in an infusion of fresh bay leaf, with sliced potatoes, tiny broad beans, and black olive slivers—no more, no less. His scallop and crayfish soup mixes mushrooms, chervil, and shrimp in a subtle brew whose secret addition, for both flavor and texture, is pigs' ears. Even in his gala creations, his use of luxury ingredients still respects the principle of simplicity and remains inspired by traditional fare: thus his scallop risotto, cooked in champagne with two kinds of

truffles and twenty-five-year-old Parmesan. Always there is a perfect balance of savors and textures, carefully controlled—balance, too, between the familiar and the marvelous.

It is this magic equilibrium between rusticity and refinement that lets Jacques Chibois represent the best of contemporary southern cuisine. And what is more, he has fun doing it. His cherub's smile reappears on the plate in a dessert like his palm tree: The fronds are created from grapefruit sections (roasted with mountain honey). Dates appropriately provide the stem, coconut sherbet the clouds, and a green apple purée provides the base. It works as well in the mouth as for the eye.

What could be simpler, and at the same time wittier, than a dessert minestrone, with mangoes, carrots, wild strawberries, basil, and savory in a heavenly broth?

Meticulous as he is, Chibois is fascinated by technique, by the chemistry and physics of the kitchen. He prefers those methods that transform food with the least violence. He feels that red meat, for instance, must be seared quickly to seal in the juices, but after that must be handled very gently. He only partially cooks beef or lamb in the oven, then puts it aside, covered, to finish cooking by itself, except for a brief reheating. Chibois also admires the old-fashioned way of cooking very fat farm birds by putting them into a cold oven and roasting them very slowly. He claims (as do all his colleagues) that fat is necessary for flavor, but food should not be heavy with fat or it will be wearying as well as unhealthy. The chef's job is to find the right balance. As for diets, he considers that food should be part of a general life hygiene, including as much variety as possible without excess.

Now, at the Bastide de Saint-Antoine, Chibois has been able to design his vast kitchen (roughly a thousand square feet of floor space) exactly as he wants it. It is meant to be visited, not hidden away from the public. Set in the back corner of the massive rectangular building and illuminated with natural light from large windows, the kitchen opens directly onto the two large dining rooms with fireplaces, beautiful tile floors, and carved woodwork. One of these rooms is linked to the sheltered, paved, outdoor terrace by two high arches, the doors of which can be opened or not as weather permits. In summer, tables are set outside under the spreading mulberry by the old stone well or in a far corner under the still denser shade of a giant horse chestnut (buckeye) tree. The entire façade is covered with an immense bougainvillea, flanked by a quite rare, red-trumpeted bignonia and old roses. Opposite, the panoramic view encompasses a broad expanse of Mediterranean beyond rolling hills. At the same time, there is easy access on the fast highway from both Grasse and Cannes, and from the six nearby golf courses! The setting combines the best of old, rural Provence with modern convenience, a certain, traditional "art of living" with contemporary invention and creativity: indeed the ideal place for Jacques Chibois. The following menu provides an excellent example of this art.

•

FISH WITH GREEN ONION BROTH
Poisson au jus d'oignon nouveau

One of Chibois' most popular (and most typical) recipes, this dish uses only five ingredients, besides the fish. Dried fennel twigs are traditionally used to flavor fish in Provence, either put in the cavity of a whole fish prepared for baking or as a bed underneath, as here. These twigs are simply the stems rather than the leaves or seeds of common fennel. Seeds could be substituted. Asparagus spears are a suggested garnish for this dish. Simple, firm, yellow-fleshed boiled potatoes can also accompany it, or for a more elaborate garnish, use rosemary-stuffed vegetables such as fennel hearts, mushroom caps, or zucchini flowers. Any high quality, small white fish is suitable, such as rex sole, sand dabs, or plaice.
SERVES 4

4 small whole white fish (about 10 ounces each), scaled and cleaned
Salt and freshly ground black pepper, to taste
Olive oil, as needed (about 1/3 cup)
Small bunch of dried fennel twigs or 1 teaspoon dried fennel seeds
4 ounces green onions, finely chopped
1 cup chicken broth or stock (store-bought or page 155)
2 cloves garlic, minced
Juice of 2 lemons

Cooked fresh asparagus spears (optional), for garnish

Preheat the oven to 450°F. Season the fish and rub them with olive oil. Rub also generously with olive oil a baking pan just big enough to hold them, and spread the fennel twigs or seeds in it. Lay the fish carefully on the twigs and bake until just cooked, about 10 minutes.

In a small skillet, heat 2 tablespoons of olive oil over medium-high heat, then add the onions. Let them cook without coloring for a few minutes, then add the chicken broth, garlic, salt, and pepper. Simmer until reduced by half.

When the fish are cooked, gently transfer them to a heated serving plate. Remove the fennel twigs and scrape the bottom of the skillet to release the brown bits. If using fennel seeds, strain the juices. Beat the juices into the onion broth along with the lemon juice. Adjust the seasoning and pour the sauce over the fish. Arrange the asparagus around them.

•

ROAST SQUAB WITH CUMIN-SPICED, OLIVE POLENTA, BRAISED CARROTS, AND FAVA BEANS
Pigeon à la polente d'olive au cumin avec sa barigoule de carottes aux fevettes

This is a simple and very colorful dish of roast pigeon or squab accompanied with polenta and an artichoke *barigoule*. Small chickens or a rabbit or Rock Cornish hens could be used instead. Polenta in Provence belongs to the indigenous traditions of Niçois cooking. The *barigoule*, like *pistou* and ratatouille, is a traditional vegetable medley that all the young chefs like to reinterpret, each in his or her own way. This recipe does not hesitate to introduce ingredients exotic for Provence: cumin and sherry. But the balance of tradition and inspiration, as of flavors and textures, is, once more, perfect.
SERVES 4

THE POLENTA
1 cup water
Salt and freshly ground black pepper, to taste
2 tablespoons polenta meal (very fine cornmeal)
1 tablespoon olive oil
1 tablespoon butter
1 teaspoon powdered cumin
15 black olives, pitted and chopped

THE BARIGOULE
2 tablespoons butter
1 medium-sized onion, minced
2 cups rich chicken broth or stock (store-bought or
*   page 155)*
1 clove garlic, minced
5 fresh sage leaves, finely chopped
6 ounces Swiss chard, ribs only, cut into fine strips
4 small artichokes, trimmed and choke removed
Salt, as needed
12 baby carrots with leaves
1 pound fresh fava beans, shelled
1/4 cup olive oil

THE SQUAB
4 squab, dressed for roasting
1 small shallot, minced
1 1/2 cups rich chicken broth or stock (store-bought
*   or page 155)*
15 black olives, pitted and chopped
1/4 cup sherry
Salt and freshly ground black pepper, to taste
3 tablespoons butter, diced
1/4 cup olive oil

Bay leaves and sprigs of fresh thyme and rosemary,
*   for garnish*

To Prepare the Polenta

Bring 1 cup salted water to a boil in a medium-sized saucepan and sprinkle the cornmeal into it. Stir until thickened, then cover and cook on very low heat for 20 to 30 minutes, stirring very often. Spoon in 1 tablespoon olive oil, 1 tablespoon butter, the cumin, and the chopped black olives. Keep warm.

To Prepare the Barigoule

Melt 2 tablespoons butter in a medium-sized skillet over medium heat and add the minced onion. Cook without coloring for a few minutes. Stir in the chicken broth, garlic, sage, chard ribs, and artichokes. Bring to a boil and simmer, uncovered, letting the mixture reduce and thicken, about 20 minutes.

In a medium-sized saucepan of boiling salted water, cook the carrots until crisp tender (5 to 7 minutes). Remove with a slotted spoon and dip into a bowl of ice water. Reserve. In the same pan, blanch the beans 4 to 5 minutes, then dip into ice water. Remove and peel. Add the carrots and the beans to the artichoke mixture and stir in the olive oil.

To Prepare the Squab

Preheat the oven to 450°F. Put the squab in a roasting pan that can also go directly on a burner and is just large enough to hold them. Roast 20 minutes. Transfer them to a warm plate, cover loosely with aluminum foil, and let them sit another 15 minutes.

Put the roasting pan over medium heat, add the minced shallot, and let brown 2 to 3 minutes. Add the broth, chopped olives, sherry, salt, and pepper. Stir and scrape the pan to release bits of meat. Beat in the butter and olive oil to thicken slightly, without letting the sauce come to a boil.

To Serve

Arrange the polenta on a platter or 4 individual dishes, with the squabs sitting on it and the vegetables spread around. Spoon over the sauce and serve the rest separately. Decorate with the bay leaves and sprigs of thyme and rosemary.

•

ORANGE SORBET WITH BASIL SAUCE
Sorbet à l'orange sauce basilic

Oranges are one of the most common of country ingredients on the French Riviera, growing in everybody's back garden. In 1857, an English tourist observed with excitement that local cows were fed on nothing so vulgar as grass, turnips, or cabbages but quite simply on oranges! Around Grasse, on terraced hillsides like those surrounding the Bastide de Saint-Antoine, citrus orchards have been set out since the Renaissance under the protecting crowns of higher olive trees, not for their fruit but for their blossoms, which were used in the perfume industry. Be sure to allow ample time for the sorbet to freeze. This dessert is stunning served in black dishes, if you have them.

SERVES 4

THE SORBET
2 cups fresh orange juice
Juice of ¹/2 lemon
4 to 6 tablespoons sugar, to taste

THE SAUCE
3 sprigs fresh basil
¹/4 cup whipping cream
1 teaspoon sugar
¹/2 teaspoon cornstarch
1 teaspoon water
Few drops fresh lemon juice

Fresh mint leaves, for garnish

To Prepare the Sorbet

In a medium-sized bowl, mix together all the ingredients for the sorbet. Pour into a sherbet maker and freeze according to the manufacturer's directions.

To Prepare the Sauce and Serve

Remove the basil leaves from the stems and reserve leaves. Put the stems, cream, and sugar in a small saucepan and heat to the boiling point. Reduce heat and simmer 5 to 6 minutes. Strain through a fine strainer and return to the pan.

In a small bowl, mix the cornstarch with I teaspoon water and add a tablespoon of the strained cream, little by little, stirring constantly. When well blended, whisk the mixture into the sauce in the pan. Roughly chop the basil leaves and add them to the pan with a few drops of lemon juice. Bring gently to a boil, stirring all the time. As soon as the sauce has slightly thickened, set the pan in a bowl of ice water to cool quickly, so that the taste and color of the basil will not be altered.

To serve, spoon some sauce into each of 6 dishes and arrange scoops of sorbet on them. Decorate with mint leaves.

Kitchen Basics

Ingredients, Sources, Basic Recipes, and Techniques

Most ingredients used in Provençal cooking are now readily available in the United States, but in some cases such as seafood, susbtitutions have been suggested. A few rarities such as fresh foie gras and squid-ink pasta may have to be ordered specially by direct mail, and suppliers addresses are furnished here. Also following are some basic recipes for stocks, pastries, and the like to supplement the chefs' recipes. Usually store-bought equivalents are available for those who prefer, and of course each cook may have his or her favorite recipe.

SEAFOOD

Rouget or red mullet is not widely available in the United States. Hawaiian goatfish (*weke ula*) is close in texture and flavor. Both the true red snapper from the Gulf of Mexico and the Pacific snapper could be used in recipes for *rouget*. And in many cases, any favorite fish with a definite flavor could be chosen. True sole (often referred to as English or Dover sole although fished also in the Mediterranean) is not found in American waters. Several types of flounder are marketed as sole in the United States, but their quality varies enormously from type to type. Petrale sole and the small rex sole and sand dabs are the best choices from Pacific waters, gray sole or lemon sole from the Atlantic.

HERBS

The new Provençal cuisine generally calls for fresh herbs except for thyme and bay leaf. Dried herbs can often be substituted in a pinch, if they are not more than six months old, by using one-third of the amount required fresh in the recipe. (One tablespoon dried herbs, for example, should be substituted for three tablespoons fresh).

ARTICHOKES

The Provençal variety of artichoke is smaller, tinged with violet, thinner, and more pointed than the common globe artichoke, which in France is a specialty of Brittany. In most recipes in this book, very small spring or baby artichokes are called for. If they are young enough, they have no choke (the inner clump of thistles). But if they are older, the choke should be removed with a spoon before using and the tough outer leaves trimmed.

FRESH DUCK FOIE GRAS

A national wholesaler is Hudson Valley Foie Gras, R.R. I, Box 69, Ferndale, NY 12734. Tel: (914) 292-2500. Fax: (914) 292-3009. They can advise you where to purchase locally. Fresh foie gras is sold nationally by mail order by Sonoma Foie Gras, P.O. Box 2007, Sonoma, CA 95476. Tel: (800) 427-4559. Fax: (707) 938-0496.

SQUID INK PASTA

Available from Gaston Dupré, 7904 Hopi Place, Tampa, FL 33634. Tel: (813) 885-9445.

WINTER WHEAT, TAPENADE, AND PROVENÇAL OLIVE OILS

Available from French Country Imports, Dany Burman, Dany Bruder Inc., 2324 Shorewood Drive, Carmichael, CA 95608. Tel: (916) 485-2103. Fax: (916) 483-1826. Other Provençal specialties can be special-ordered through this company.

PUFF PASTRY

Allow two hours for the preparation. Use a chilled bowl and work as much as possible in a cool place so that the butter will not get too soft. It should ideally have and keep the same consistency as the flour and water dough. The idea is to trap the butter between multiple layers of pastry that should never be allowed to tear during the folding. This is one of the most difficult pastries to make successfully for the home cook, but good, store-bought puff pastry is available in most areas, both fresh at French bakeries and frozen at better supermarkets. Leftover dough and scraps may be cut into rectangles, circles, or diamond shapes and baked for garnishes or for canapés. YIELD: 12 OUNCES, enough for one 9-inch pie.

1 1/4 cup all-purpose flour plus more as needed for rolling out
1/2 cold cup water or as needed
Pinch of salt
1 stick (1/4 pound) chilled unsalted butter

Put the flour into a medium-sized mixing bowl and make a well in the center. Pour in a scant 1/2 cup water and add the salt. Mix with a wooden spatula. Add more water if necessary to make a firm dough, then turn out onto a lightly floured surface and knead lightly until smooth and elastic, several times. Return to the bowl and chill 15 minutes. Flour the surface again if necessary and rub flour onto the rolling pin. Lay out the pastry in a square about 1/3 inch thick. Cut 1/3 of the cold butter into small pieces and spread these evenly over the pastry. Fold the 4 corners of the pastry inwards to cover completely the butter. Pat flat. Then fold the left 1/3 of the pastry toward the center, repeat with the right 1/3 to make 3 layers. With the rolling pin, roll the pastry again to a thickness of 1/3 inch. Wrap in plastic wrap and chill 15 minutes.

Repeat the entire operation 2 more times: spreading bits of butter, folding in the 4 corners, then folding into 3 layers, rolling out to a 1/3-inch layer.

Cut or roll into whatever shape required by the recipe, and cook according to recipe directions.

SWEET OR SAVORY PASTRY SHELLS

A simple, family piecrust recipe. Makes enough for one 9-inch pie shell or four 4-inch shells.

1 1/4 cup flour
Pinch of salt
Pinch of sugar (for a sweet filling)
1 stick (1/4 pound) butter, cold but not hard
About 1/2 cup cold water

Mix the flour with the salt and sugar (if using) in a medium-sized bowl. Add the butter in small bits and quickly work it into the flour with your fingertips until it is well mixed and remains in pieces the size of small peas. Handle it as little as possible. Add half the water, then more as necessary to mix the dough into a ball that sticks together.

Lightly flour the working surface. Break off bits of dough and rub it into the surface with the heel of your hand so that the butter smears into the flour. Continue until all the dough has been treated in this way, about 2 minutes. Form a ball again, scraping it with a knife from the work surface if necessary. Handle the dough as little as possible throughout. Cover with plastic wrap and chill 15 minutes. If a finger poked into the dough leaves its original mark, the pastry is ready to use. If the dough bounces back and eliminates the finger mark, then it needs to rest longer.

Roll out dough to 1/4 inch thick for piecrust. Lay a sheet of pastry gently over the greased pie pan and press it into place, taking care not to break or damage it. There should be a slight overhang all around the plate. Then with an even pressure, run the rolling pin back and forth over the pie plate in such a way that the pastry overhang falls neatly away and the pie shell is ready to fill or bake empty. (If the latter, fill the dish with a layer of dried beans to keep the crust in place during the baking.) Oven temperature and cooking times will vary depending on whether the shell is empty or filled and the type of filling.

For individual pastry shells, preheat the oven to 425°F. Roll out the pastry in as even a square as possible and cut into 4 equal parts. Proceed with each pie tin as indicated above for a single large one. Place a layer of dried beans in the bottom of each shell and bake until golden, about 10 minutes.

THICK CUSTARD OR PASTRY CREAM

Any custard cream not required for the recipe may be frozen for later use. Thinned with a little half-and-half, it can make a dessert cream. Or the custard can be served in baked pie shells, topped with seasonal fruit.
MAKES ABOUT 2 CUPS

2 cups milk
1 vanilla bean, split, or 1 teaspoon vanilla extract
2 whole eggs and 1 egg yolk
1/2 cup sugar
3 tablespoons all-purpose flour

In a small saucepan, scald the milk with the vanilla over medium heat. Remove, strain if a bean has been used, and reserve. In a medium-sized bowl, beat the eggs and yolk, add sugar, beat again, then mix in the flour.

Pour the contents of the bowl into the top of a double boiler. Heat gently over simmering water. Gradually stir in the warm milk, and cook, stirring constantly, until the custard just reaches the point of boiling. Remove from the heat and keep stirring so that there will be no film formed on the top. Cover and chill before using.

VANILLA ICE CREAM
MAKES ABOUT 1 PINT

1 cup milk
1 cup heavy cream
1/2 cup sugar
1 vanilla bean, split
6 egg yolks

Scald the milk, cream, 1/4 cup of the sugar, and the vanilla bean in the top of a double boiler over simmering water. In a medium-sized bowl, beat the egg yolks until thick. Pour the hot milk mixture onto them, little by little, stirring constantly, until well blended. Return the contents of the bowl to the double boiler and cook over low heat until thickened slightly. Do not let it boil. Strain the mixture and freeze it in an ice-cream maker, according to the manufacturer's directions.

TO ROAST BELL OR CHILI PEPPERS
Preheat the oven to 500°F. Place whole peppers on an oiled baking sheet and place in the oven, turning frequently, until the skins are well scorched. Remove them from the oven and rinse under cold running water. The skins should rub off easily. Dry and cut in half. Remove seeds, membranes, and stems.

Alternatively, peppers may be grilled on a fork over a gas flame, turning regularly until the outside is evenly scorched.

TO MAKE SUGAR SYRUP
Mix in a large saucepan 4 cups water and 3¾ cups granulated sugar. Stir to dissolve, and heat slowly to the boiling point. Simmer, uncovered and without stirring, for 10 minutes. Remove from heat and let cool.
MAKES 1 QUART

TO MAKE STOCK OR BROTH FROM FISH, CHICKEN, RABBIT, OR MEAT BONES
Place the bones in a small to large saucepan, depending on their volume. Just barely cover with water. For extra flavor, a bay leaf and a sprig of thyme, 1 chopped carrot, and 1 chopped onion can be added to the bones in the pan. Season with salt and pepper. Bring to a boil and simmer half an hour for fish, rabbit, or chicken bones, an hour for lamb. Degrease if necessary by tipping the pan and spooning out the fat into a small bowl. Strain and use in the recipe.

Alternatively, chicken or meat stock can be prepared a day ahead, strained into a bowl, covered, and chilled. This will make it easy to remove the fat in a solid layer from the top before using the stock in a recipe. Fish stock, however, should be made just before using.

TO ROAST HAZELNUTS
Preheat the oven to 400°F. Spread the hazelnuts on a baking sheet and roast them in the oven until golden, stirring to turn from time to time, about 10 minutes. Let cool, then rub nuts together to remove the skins. Blend or grind into a fine powder or chop roughly with a sharp knife, according to desired use.

Afterword

FRANÇOIS MILLO ON THE WINES OF PROVENCE

Grapevines originated in the Middle East, but arrived in Provence with the Greeks who founded Marseille some 2600 years ago. The following centuries saw the vineyards of Provence expand and evolve, reaching a peak of heightened activity as we approach the year 2000.

Starting in the mid-twentieth century, intensive replanting has made particular use of the following grape varieties: Syrah, Grenache, Mourvèdre and Cabernet for the reds; Sémillon, Ugni Blanc, and a remarkable local variety, Rolle, for the whites.

Techniques and equipment have changed radically in recent decades, as have the vintners. Always open to the outside world, Provence has recently welcomed many new vintners from other regions and countries, who adopt local traditions and lifestyles, but who bring new ideas and inspiration.

The relatively poor soil of Provence is ideal for producing quality wines, bathed in Mediterranean sunlight. Dry, cool winters and abundant spring rains give the vines a good start. Dry, hot summers rapidly mature the grapes, and harvesting generally takes place before the bad weather of autumn. The mistral, a strong, drying north wind that can be cold in winter, keeps the vineyards healthy.

So it is that drought, sun, and wind combine to make the wine of Provence one of the most natural in France. Its grapes require very little spraying and no artificial improvement.

The wines of Provence come from two main areas: The lower Rhône valley, north of Avignon to the Mediterranean, produces the southern Côtes du Rhône. These are largely strong, tannic red wines. The soil, climate, and grape varieties chosen, as well as the methods of vinification, make these wines particularly well suited to aging in oak casks.

The best known of these Rhône wines is Châteauneuf du Pape, but appellations such as Gigondas, Vacqueras, Costières de Nîmes, or the Côtes du Ventoux also reveal the extremely varied personality of these arid slopes. These wines ideally accompany red meat, game, and cheese. They particularly suit traditional French cuisine.

The second section, less well known, covers most of Mediterranean Provence. This area includes eight different appellations: Coteaux d'Aix, Côtes du Lubéron, Palette, Cassis, Bandol, Coteaux Varois, Côtes de Provence, and Bellet. Each has its own character, it own specialities: the whites of Cassis, the reds of Bandol, the rosés of the Côtes de Provence. These wines demonstrate the same diversity and strong personality that characterizes the region and its inhabitants.

Although best known for its rosés, the Mediterranean part of Provence today offers quality wines in all

three colors: Lively and fruity reds can accompany outdoor grilled food cooked with Provençal herbs; or, when
allowed to mature, they will go with cheese and game.
The whites when young are ideal with local seafood, but
can also wait several years to accompany white meat and
certain cheeses.

The rosé remains the star: a delicate wine that is
often misunderstood. Its vinification is an art mastered
over centuries. The rosé of Provence takes on its salmon
color, its characteristic brilliance, and its other qualities
in only a few hours, during a short maceration. This pro-

cessing of red grapes requires total and infallible mastery.

Served as an aperitif, these rosés awaken the taste
buds, but leave the palate open for the meal that follows.
They can be as elegant as the grandest wines, to accompany rare dishes, just as they can accompany exotic cuisine or simply equal the diversity of local fare.

Grown from ancient traditions into wines of strong
and original character, today's production of the Côtes
de Provence appellations maintains its sincerity and au-
thenticity. Lovers of the new Provençal cuisine find these
wines ideally natural and light, simple but refined.

SOME WHITE VARIETIES USED IN PROVENCE WINES

Rolle:
Grown in this region by the ancient Ligurians, this grape is both robust and subtly flavored. Used more and more today, it produces wines with citrus and pear overtones, fine bodied and aromatic.

Ugni Blanc:
Vigorous and upright, this vinestock produces round, juicy grapes and light, fruity wines. A careful limitation of its production and the use of new techniques of vinification have increased their delicacy.

Clairette:
A very old Provençal variety suited to poor soil, producing little in quantity. Its oblong grapes yield heady, aromatic wines with a rich bouquet.

Sémillon:
This vigorous grape is productive but susceptible to disease. It nonetheless adds a certain elegance to the white Côtes de Provence, when used in small quantities.

SOME RED VARIETIES USED IN PROVENCE WINES

Syrah:
Originally from Spain, this variety is harvested later than others and gives solid, strongly colored, rough wines ready to drink early on because of their high proportion of tannins, but is particularly suited to long aging. Through the years, wines made with Syrah develop echoes of vanilla, Havana tobacco, and red fruits (strawberry, raspberry, red currant).

Grenache:
This variety constitutes the basis for the Côtes de Provence and produces powerful wines, high in alcoholic content, rich, and round.

Carignan:
Cultivated on hilly ground for wines produced in small amounts, which are well structured and colorful. The grape also provides an excellent basis for mixing with other varieties.

Cinsault:
The beauty and taste of these grapes is such that they have long been grown for the table. But the wine they produce is fresh and fruity and adds subtlety when mixed with other varieties.

Tivouren:
Provençal originally, this variety contributes particularly to the production of rosé wines. Its delicate aroma and rich bouquet makes it an elegant but discrete partner.

Mourvèdre:
Also southern French in its origins, this excellent variety produces small, closely bunched grapes and a colorful, well-balanced wine. Its smooth texture develops through aging, for which it is particularly well suited.

Cabernet Sauvignon:
Little used in Provence, this grape adds a strong tannic note and allows for long aging. Its characteristic aroma of green bell pepper distinguishes it from the other varieties.

—François Millo
*Director of the Interprofessional Committee
of the Côtes de Provence*

RENÉ BERGÈS.
Relais Sainte-Victoire,
13100 Beaurecueil
Tel: 42 66 94 98
Fax: 42 66 85 96

ELISABETH BOURGEOIS.
Le Mas Tourteron,
Les Imberts, 84220 Gordes
Tel: 90 72 00 16
Fax: 90 72 09 81

FRANCIS CARDAILLAC.
Restaurant L'Olivier,
La Bastide de Saint-Tropez,
83990 Saint-Tropez
Tel: 94 97 58 16
Fax: 94 97 21 71

JEAN-ANDRÉ CHARIAL.
Oustau de Baumanière
(Relais & Châteaux),
13520 Les Baux-de-Provence
Tel: 90 54 33 07
Fax: 90 54 40 46

SERGE CHENET.
Le Prieuré (Relais & Châteaux),
7, place du Chapitre,
30400 Villeneuve-lez-Avignon
Tel: 90 25 18 20
Fax: 90 25 45 39

JACQUES CHIBOIS.
La Bastide de Saint-Antoine,
avenue Henri Dunant,
Quartier Saint-Antoine,
06300 Grasse

CHRISTIAN ETIENNE.
Restaurant Christian Etienne,
10, rue de Mons,
84000 Avignon
Tel: 90 86 16 50
Fax: 90 86 67 09

JEAN-CLAUDE GUILLON.
Grand Hôtel du Cap-Ferrat,
71, avenue Général de Gaulle,
06290 Saint-Jean-Cap-Ferrat
Tel: 93 76 50 50
Fax: 93 76 04 52

PHILIPPE MONTI.
Hostellerie de Crillon-le-Brave,
place de l'Eglise,
84410 Crillon-le-Brave
Tel: 90 65 61 61
Fax: 90 65 62 86
Owners: Peter Chittick
and Craig Miller

PASCAL MOREL.
L'Abbaye de Sainte-Croix
(Relais & Châteaux),
13300 Salon-de-Provence
Tel: 90 56 24 55
Fax: 90 56 31 12
Owner: Catherine Bossard

ALAIN NICOLET.
Restaurant Alain Nicolet,
B.P. 28, route de Pertuis,
84460 Cheval-Blanc
Tel: 90 78 01 56
Fax: 90 71 91 28

JACQUES AND
LAURENT POURCEL.
Le Jardin des Sens,
11, avenue Saint-Lazare,
34400 Montpellier
Tel: 67 79 63 38
Fax: 67 72 13 05

RAYMOND ROSSO.
Les Arcenaulx,
25, cours d'Estienne d'Orves,
13001 Marseille
Tel: 91 54 39 37
Fax: 91 54 76 33
Owners: Jeanne
and Simone Laffitte

REINE SAMMUT.
La Fénière,
9, rue du Grand Pré,
84160 Lourmarin
Tel: 90 68 11 79
Fax: 90 68 18 60

LAURENT TARRIDEC.
Hôtel Les Roches,
1, avenue des Trois Dauphins,
Aiguebelle Plage,
83980 Le Lavandou
Tel: 94 71 05 07
Fax: 94 71 08 40
New Address 1995:
Bistrot des Lices,
83990 Saint Tropez
Tel: 94 97 29 00
Fax: 94 97 76 39

Bibliography

Blume, Mary. *Côte d'Azur: Inventing the French Riviera.*
London: Thames and Hudson, 1992.

Bosco, Henri. *Le Mas Théotime.*
Paris: Gallimard, 1952.

_____. Le Trestoulas.
Paris: Gallimard, 1935.

Bossieu, Jean. *Les Arcenaulx de Marseille.*
Marseille: Association Culturelle, Les Arcenaulx, 1980.

Brink, André. *The Wall of the Plague.*
London: Fontana, 1985.

Cameron, Roderick. *The Golden Riviera.*
Honolulu: Editions Limited, 1975.

Colette. *La Naissance du jour.*
Paris: Garnier-Flammarion, 1969.

_____. *Prisons et paradis.*
Paris: Fayard, 1986.

_____. *La Vagabonde.*
Paris: Albin Michel, 1973.

Conversations avec Cézanne. Critical edition, edited by
P. M. Doran.
Paris: Editions Macula, 1978.

Daudet, Alphonse. *Lettres de mon moulin.*
Paris: Fasquelle, 1970.

David, Elizabeth. *An Omelette and a Glass of Wine.*
Middlesex, England: Penguin, 1984.

Davidson, Alan. *Mediterranean Seafood.*
Middlesex, England: Penguin, 1972.

Durrell, Lawrence. *Spirit of Place: Letters and Essays
on Travel.*
New Haven, Conn.: Leete's Island Books, 1969.

Escoffier, Auguste. *Souvenirs inédits.*
Marseille: Editions Jeanne Lafitte, 1985.

Fisher, M.F.K. *Two Towns in Provence.*
New York: Random House, Vintage Books, 1983.

Forbes, Leslie. *A Taste of Provence.*
Boston: Little Brown and Co., 1988.

Ford, Ford Madox. *Provence.*
New York: Ecco Press, 1979.

Giono, Jean. *Manosque-des-Plateaux suivi de Poème de l'olive.*
Paris: Gallimard, 1986.

Howarth, Patrick. *When the Riviera Was Ours.*
London: Century, 1977.

Jacobs, Michael. *A Guide to Provence.*
London: Viking Penguin, 1988.

James, Henry. *A Little Tour in France.*
Oxford: Oxford University Press, 1984.

Jouveau, René. *La Cuisine provençal de tradition populaire.*
Nîmes, France: Imprimerie Bene, 1976.

Krantz, Judith. *Mistral's Daughter.*
New York: Bantam, 1983.

"Le Goût à la Carte." *Gault-Millau Magazine.* 278
(October 1992).

Mayle, Peter. *A Year in Provence.*
London: Hamish Hamilton, 1989.

Médecin, Jacques. *Cuisine Niçoise.*
Middlesex, England: Penguin, 1972.

Mistral, Frédéric. *The Memoirs of Frédéric Mistral.*
Translated by George Wickes.
New York: New Directions, 1986.

Pickvance, Ronald. *Van Gogh in Arles.*
New York: Metropolitan Museum of Art, 1984.

Pope-Hennessy, James. *Aspects of Provence.*
London: Penguin Travel Library, 1988.

Reboul, J.-B. *La Cuisinière provençale.*
Marseille: Tacussel, 1903.

Root, Waverley. *The Food of France.*
New York: Random House, Vintage Books, 1977.

Sainte-Victoire Cézanne 1990 (catalogue exhibit).
Aix-en-Provence: Réunion des musées nationaux, 1990.

Serguier, Clément. *Pour un panier de figues.*
Avignon, France: A. Barthelemy, 1992.

Stendhal. *Mémoires d'un touriste: Voyage dans le Midi.*
Paris: Maspéro, 1981.

Thompson, David. *Petrarch: An Anthology.*
New York: Harper and Row, 1971.

Van Gogh, Vincent. *The Letters of Vincent Van Gogh.*
Edited by Mark Roskill.
New York: Atheneum, 1963.

INDEX

INDEX

TABLE OF EQUIVALENTS

The exact equivalents in the following tables have been rounded for convenience.

US/UK

oz=ounce
lb=pound
in=inch
ft=foot
tbl=tablespoon
fl oz=fluid ounce
qt=quart

METRIC

g=gram
kg=kilogram
mm=millimeter
cm=centimeter
ml=milliliter
l=liter

WEIGHTS

US/UK	Metric
1 oz	30 g
2 oz	60 g
3 oz	90 g
4 oz (1/4 lb)	125 g
5 oz (1/3 lb)	155 g
6 oz	185 g
7 oz	220 g
8 oz (1/2 lb)	250 g
10 oz	315 g
12 oz (3/4 lb)	375 g
14 oz	440 g
16 oz (1 lb)	500 g
1 1/2 lb	750 g
2 lb	1 kg
3 lb	1.5 kg

OVEN TEMPERATURES

Fahrenheit	Celsius	Gas
250	120	1/2
275	140	1
300	150	2
325	160	3
350	180	4
375	190	5
400	200	6
425	220	7
450	230	8
475	240	9
500	260	10

LIQUIDS

US	Metric	UK
2 tbl	30 ml	1 fl oz
1/4 cup	60 ml	2 fl oz
1/3 cup	80 ml	3 fl oz
1/2 cup	125 ml	4 fl oz
2/3 cup	160 ml	5 fl oz
3/4 cup	180 ml	6 fl oz
1 cup	250 ml	8 fl oz
1 1/2 cups	375 ml	12 fl oz
2 cups	500 ml	16 fl oz
4 cups/1 qt	1 l	32 fl oz

LENGTH MEASURES

1/8 in	3 mm
1/4 in	6 mm
1/2 in	12 mm
1 in	2.5 cm
2 in	5 cm
3 in	7.5 cm
4 in	10 cm
5 in	13 cm
6 in	15 cm
7 in	18 cm
8 in	20 cm
9 in	23 cm
10 in	25 cm
11 in	28 cm
12/1 ft	30 cm